LEGAL AND CONTRACTUAL
PROCEDURES
FOR ARCHITECTS

FOURTH EDITION

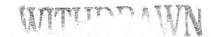

BY

Bob Greenstreet
and
David Chappell

with additional material
by
KAREN GREENSTREET

Architectural Press
An imprint of Butterworth-Heinemann
Linacre House, Jordan Hill, Oxford OX2 8DP
225 Wildwood Avenue, Woburn, MA 01801-2041
A division of Reed Educational and Professional Publishing Ltd

Ⓡ A member of the Reed Elsevier plc group

OXFORD   AUCKLAND   BOSTON
JOHANNESBURG   MELBOURNE   NEW DELHI

First published 1981
Second edition 1984
Third edition 1989
Fourth edition 1994
Reprinted 1996, 1998, 1999

British Library Cataloguing in Publication Data
Greenstreet, Bob
    Legal and Contractual Procedures for
    Architects. - 4Rev.ed
    I. Title II. Chappell, David
    344.2037869

ISBN 0 7506 1617 2

Library of Congress Cataloguing in Publication Data
Greenstreet, Bob
    Legal and Contractual Procedures for
    Architects. - 4th ed./by Bob Greenstreet
    and David Chappell; with additional
    material by Karen Greenstreet
    p.   cm.
    Includes bibliographical references and index.
    ISBN 0 7506 1617 2
    1. Architectural contracts - Great Britain.
    2. Architects - Legal status, laws,etc. -
    Great Britain. I.Chappell, David.
    II. Greenstreet, Karen.   III. Title.
    KD2978.G74 1993
    344.41'0176172 - dc20
    [344.104176172]

                                              93 - 5253
                                                    CIP

Printed in Great Britain by
Athenaeum Press Ltd, Gateshead, Tyne & Wear

TABLE OF CONTENTS

PREFACE

In everyday practice, the architect spends considerable time carrying out various administrative tasks and dealing with problems and situations arising from the design and construction of each new building project. In order to do this effectively, a basic knowledge of all relevant procedures involved is necessary, coupled with an understanding of the broader legal and professional issues that are at stake.

'Legal and Contractual Procedures for Architects' provides a comprehensive, concise and simplified source of practical information, giving the reader a basic legal overview of the wider principles affecting the profession, and concentrating on the more specific procedural aspects of the architect's duties. In addition, it contains a series of checklists, diagrams and completed forms which provide a quick and easy reference source.

Each section of the book culminates with a number of problems that could face the architect, laid out on "action required" sheets. These are dealt with in the context of a simulated office scenario on the following "action taken" pages, where (to facilitate easy reading), an office diary format has been adopted. The responses on these pages are not meant to be model answers, as each problem would in reality merit its own unique handling. Rather, they are meant to convey an attitude appropriate to successful practice management. Students preparing for Part III RIBA examinations are advised to work through the book, attempting the problems themselves before checking their answers against those in the text.

The 1980 Edition Standard Form of Building Contract (Private with Quantities) incorporating Amendments 1-11 has been referred to throughout, and a commentary of its Conditions is included on pages 57 to 60. Also, many of the forms used in the book are published by the RIBA; although their use is not mandatory, they are useful in providing a consistency of understanding for all parties involved in the construction process, and are therefore recommended in most cases.

'Legal and Contractual Procedures for Architects' offers only a basic framework of information, as a detailed coverage of the numerous aspects of the subject could not possibly be crammed into 110 pages. For this reason, the text is carefully cross-referenced to other sources, both at the foot of each page, and in the final section. Lack of space has also dictated that certain matters (e.g. work in public organisations, requirements in Inner London etc.) have been excluded. Similarly, to avoid a cumbersome text, the architect has been referred to in the masculine gender thoughout.

Since the original publication of this book in 1981, there have been numerous changes in the legal, professional and administrative aspects of architecture. In consequence, a second edition was published in 1984 which substantially updated and enlarged the original text which was again revised in the third edition, published in 1989. In the preparation of the fourth edition, every attempt has been made to respond to further developments over the past four years.

Our thanks go to the following individuals:

RIBA for permission to use their documents.

KAREN GREENSTREET MA SOLICITOR for considerable assistance in the preparation of the original text, including much of the legal content, editing, referencing and indexing.

PHIL DALLOWAY DMS MIBC MIFireE MBIM and HARVEY PRITCHARD BA(Hons)DipTP MRTPI for assistance on the Building Control and Planning pages in the third edition.

IAN FEWTRELL-SMITH RIBA DipArch(Oxford) for preparation of the standard forms and checking the text in the first edition.

JOHN CANE LLB DipArch(Birmingham) RIBA FFB FCIArb FFAS for contributions to the "action required" and "action taken" pages.

It is not the intention of the authors to provide a legal service in the publication of this book, but to offer an introduction to legal and practical matters concerning architecture. Legal assistance is advised where appropriate.

SECTION ONE

THE ARCHITECT AND THE LAW

Contents | Page

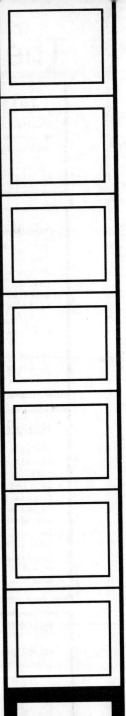

Legal
Background

The Law

Law

English Law is basically a body of rules aimed at preserving the fabric of society, and is embodied in: COMMON LAW
STATUTE LAW
EQUITY

Common Law

The basic 'rules' of society have developed through the common law, and are governed by the doctrine of 'stare decisis', constraining English judges to stand by past decisions of superior courts. Although decisions must be based on similar previous cases, the judge may still draw relevant distinctions pertinent to each new case, enabling the common law to continually develop and adapt to the changing values of society. However, where a conflict arises between the common law and a statute, the latter prevails.

Statute Law

Statutes are laws officially approved by Parliament. They are suggested by concerned parties (often a Government Ministry), prepared and laid before both the House of Lords and House of Commons in the form of a Bill, and, if approved, become Acts of Parliament. In some cases, an Act may serve as the enabling legislation, empowering more specific requirements to be made in the form of Rules, Orders or Statutory Instruments. For example, The Building Act 1984 empowered the creation of the Building Regulations 1985 (as amended) as Statutory Instruments.

Equity

Equity provides a measure of fairness or natural justice not always available under statute or common law, by allowing additional remedies and procedures based on principles of 'conscience' to supplement the law.

From a more practical standpoint, law can be classified into two branches : CRIMINAL LAW
CIVIL LAW

Criminal Law

This is public law, concerned with offences against society as a whole. e.g. robbery, murder, theft. Crimes may also be acts which, although not anti-social in a moral sense, infringe rules existing to ensure the smooth administration of the country. e.g. tax offences, certain road traffic offences. Most crimes are now covered by statutes, although several common law offences still exist. e.g. aiding and abetting.

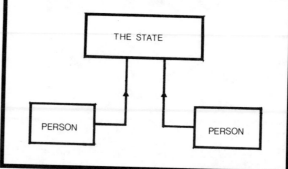

Civil Law

This is private law, concerned with the rights and obligations of individuals and corporations in their dealings with each other. It is frequently embodied in the general common law although there is an increasing tendency to enact civil law provisions. e.g. Misrepresentation Act 1967, Unfair Contract Terms Act 1977.
Matters covered by civil law provisions include : SUCCESSION
FAMILY
CONTRACT
PROPERTY
TORT
EMPLOYMENT

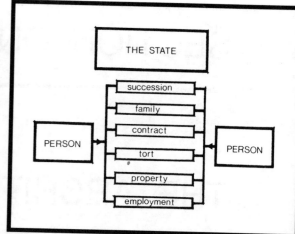

Contract & Tort

To architectural practice, the most relevant branches of civil law are :

CONTRACT LAW, which concerns the legally binding rights and obligations of parties who have made an agreement for a specific purpose (see page 54).
and
TORT, literally a 'wrong' done by one individual or corporation to another for which a remedy (e.g. compensation, injunction) may be sought. There are a number of specific torts. These include: NEGLIGENCE (see page 8)
TRESPASS (see page 38)
NUISANCE
DEFAMATION

It is possible that an action may fall under both the law of contract and tort (where, for example, a negligent act results in a breach of contract). In such a case it is sometimes easier to sue on the contract, rather than prove the tort.

R
E
F LAW MADE SIMPLE. pp.1-23
ARCHITECT'S LEGAL HANDBOOK. pp.1-2,9-10.

The Courts

For purposes of administrative expediency, different types of legal questions are dealt with in different courts. There is a wide variety of specialist courts designed to provide an efficient means of disposing of specific matters. These include :

- THE CORONER'S COURT
- THE NATIONAL INDUSTRIAL RELATIONS COURT
- THE RESTRICTIVE PRACTICES COURT

However, the courts which deal with the majority of cases in England and Wales are:

- THE COUNTY COURTS
- THE HIGH COURT
- THE MAGISTRATES' COURTS
- THE CROWN COURTS

The relationship and hierarchies within the criminal and civil court structures can be best illustrated in diagram form :

Criminal Court

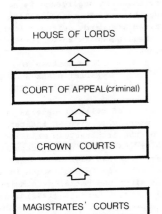

All criminal proceedings begin (and usually end) in the magistrates' court. However, more serious offences are always passed on to be tried in the Crown Courts.

Civil Court

```
            HOUSE OF LORDS
                 ⇧
         COURT OF APPEAL (civil)
                 ⇧
              HIGH COURT
    queen's bench | family | chancery
                 ⇧
            COUNTY COURTS      appeal
```

Proceedings in civil law may begin in either the county court or the High Court, depending

    a) on the type of matter and

    b) on the financial amount involved.

Generally, the less financially consequential cases are heard in the county courts.

Appeal from the county court is not via the High Court, but directly to the Court of Appeal. In all civil court proceedings, legal representation is advisable, though not always strictly necessary.

Standard of Proof

This is higher in criminal proceedings than in civil cases. In the former, the prosecution must prove its case against the defendant 'beyond a reasonable doubt', whereas in civil matters, the plaintiff bears the burden of proving his allegations, after which the judge will decide the verdict upon a 'balance of probabilities'.

Other means available for the resolution of disputes include :

    ARBITRATION (see page 95).

    ALTERNATIVE DISPUTE RESOLUTION (see page 98)

    SPECIAL TRIBUNALS, which tend to be less formal than the courts, and may be set up to reconcile the individual's rights with statutory demands enacted ostensibly to protect him.

Small Claims

Less formal procedures exist for individuals wishing to sue for sums less than £1,000 in the county court. Small claims can be dealt with within the county court structure, but without legal representation, where the facts of the case are considered usually (but not always) by the District Judge. The main advantage of the small claims procedure is that it enables anyone to sue for a relatively small amount without incurring legal costs which otherwise might easily exceed the claim itself.

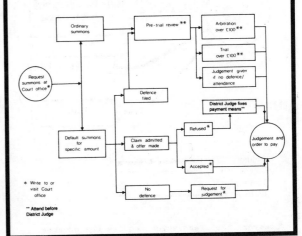

* Write to or visit Court office

** Attend before District Judge

In most legal matters affecting architectural practice, it is advisable to take legal advice before proceeding. There are various sources available : A SOLICITOR

    THE LOCAL LAW CENTRE

    CITIZEN'S ADVICE BUREAU

    CONSUMER ADVICE BUREAU

Legal aid may be available in civil matters, but only at the discretion of the regional administration of the Legal Aid Fund.

REF | SMALL CLAIMS IN THE COUNTY COURTS (available from all county courts)
LAW MADE SIMPLE. pp. 24-62, 81-87.

The Architects Liability

The architect's legal obligations and responsibilities are governed by both statute and common law:

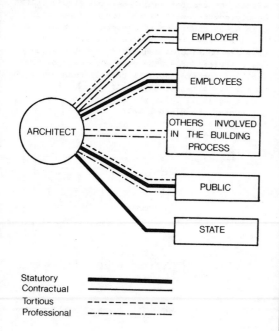

EMPLOYER

EMPLOYEES

OTHERS INVOLVED IN THE BUILDING PROCESS

ARCHITECT

PUBLIC

STATE

Statutory ▬▬▬
Contractual ────
Tortious ─ ─ ─ ─
Professional ─·─·─·

However, the areas which require the greatest attention are:
- BREACH OF CONTRACT
- NEGLIGENCE

Breach of Contract

The architect is not a party to the Standard Form, but has a separate contractual relationship with the employer (see page 21). In this, he agrees to carry out the work with reasonable skill and care. Failure to meet these standards will be in breach of the contract and if it results in problems causing extra expense or delays, the architect will be liable for damages.

Negligence

Outside the discernible contractual obligations imposed by the contract exists a duty under the law of torts (see page 6), particularly in negligence. The architect may be liable for the consequences arising from his negligent behaviour, even where no contractual relationship exists.

The extent to which anyone may be held liable to others in tort depends on the DUTY OF CARE that is owed. In contractual situations, the liability of both parties is defined, but in tort, it is often difficult to determine the existence or extent of the duty of care. However, the law provides some guidance in certain circumstances by defining certain liabilities. The more important of these include: STRICT LIABILITY
OCCUPIER'S LIABILITY
EMPLOYER'S LIABILITY
VICARIOUS LIABILITY

A. Strict

This applies in certain cases where liability may exist independently of wrongful intent or negligence. An illustration of this rule exists in *RYLANDS v FLETCHER 1868*, where water from a reservoir flooded the mineshaft on neighbouring property and led to a successful claim for damages, although no negligent act was proved. The decision against the reservoir owner was made on the basis that he had kept on his land 'something likely to do mischief', and that it had subsequently 'escaped'.

B. Occupier's

Under the Occupier's Liability Act 1957, an occupier of premises owes a duty of care to all lawful visitors to those premises.

C. Employer's

An employer may be liable for injury caused to his employees by acts of negligence of his fellow employees acting in the course of their employment. Liability also exists if the employer breaches his statutory duty, or if the injury is caused by the employer's negligence.

D. Vicarious

This may exist in certain limited circumstances where one party becomes responsible for certain acts of another without necessarily contributing to the negligence. The most common example of vicarious liability is an employer's responsibility for the acts of his employees.

Regarding responsibility to third parties, certain conditions must be shown to allow a claim for negligent behaviour to be successful. It must be shown:

- That a duty of care to the injured party existed at the time of the injury.

- That there was a breach of this duty.

- That the injured party suffered damage or loss as a result of the breach.

Standard of Care

In all cases, it is the REASONABLE STANDARD OF CARE established by common law against which a defendant party's performance will be judged. "Liability based in negligence is not necessarily blameworthiness. It means falling short of a court's fixed standards, often a standard of perfects. Negligence is an arbitrary and uncertain concept".

Lord Monkman in
HEDLEY BYRNE & CO LTD v
HELLER & PARTNERS LTD 1964

An examination of relevant caselaw on the four following pages will give an indication of the position of the architect in relation to potentially hazardous areas in his duties where negligent behaviour has been determined.
Note that liability in negligence is more restricted since the decision in Murphy v Brentwood District Council (1990) (see page 10)

REF   LAW MADE SIMPLE. pp. 191-208, 224-236.

1

HEDLEY BYRNE & CO. LTD v HELLER & PARTNERS
LTD [1963] 2 All ER 575

- The Facts:
A bank enquired on behalf of a customer whether,
in the opinion of certain merchant bankers (the
defendants) a company, E. Ltd., was of good
financial status. The merchant bank replied that
E. Ltd. was respectably constituted, and good
for its normal business engagements. The appel-
lants relied upon these statements and subsequently suffered loss of over £17,000 as a
result of E. Ltd becoming bankrupt.
- Held:
Where in the ordinary course of business or
professional affairs a person's skill or
judgment is relied upon, and that person chooses
to give information or advice without clearly
showing that he does not accept responsibility,
that person accepts a legal duty to exercise
such care as the circumstances require in making
his reply. If he fails to exercise that degree
of care, an action for negligence will lie if
damage results.
- Comment:
Prior to this case, it was thought that a person
could be liable for negligent deeds, but not for
negligent words. The principle of negligent
misstatement arising out of Hedley Byrne was
reiterated in:
Clay v A.J. Crump & Sons [1963] - where an
architect, while inspecting a site in the course
of demolition, negligently stated that a certain
wall was safe and could remain. Subsequently,
the wall collapsed causing injury to a labourer,
and as a result the architect was held liable
for his negligent misstatement.
There is one notable exception to the general
rule laid down in Hedley Byrne: a barrister is
not liable for negligent advocacy, even where
his client suffers loss through actual misstate-
ments of the law (Rondel v Worsley [1967]).
Hedley Byrne has been recently applied, but
strictly interpreted in Caparo Industries plc v
Dickman [1990].

2

STOVIN-BRADFORD v VOLPOINT PROPERTIES LTD
& ANOTHER [1971] 3 All ER 570

- The Facts:
The plaintiff, an architect, designed and produced plans for the defendant company's proposed
warehouses, and submitted the plans for planning
permission which was subsequently granted.
The architect had heard adverse reports of the
defendants' dealings with architects, and when
submitting his account for the work (the fees
for which were considerably below RIBA scale) he
expressly reserved his copyright of the design
which was very distinctive, in that it included
an unusual and pleasing diamond-shaped feature.
The architect then withdrew from the project,
but was later surprised to notice that the
defendant company were building the warehouses
to a design which incorporated the diamond-
shaped feature.
- Held:
The defendants were liable for infringement of
the plaintiff's copyright because the fee
charged by the plaintiff was nominal, and did
not carry an implied licence to use the plans
produced, or the design concepts. Damages were
assessed on the basis of what would be a fair
fee for a licence to use the copyright in the
plans for the purpose for which it was used.
- Comment:
This case suggests that, provided RIBA recommended fees are charged, the architect grants an
implied licence to use the design. However, Lord
Justice Salmon, one of the three judges hearing
the appeal stated:

*"I am by no means convinced that even if an
architect were to charge the full scale fee for
preparing drawings for planning permission
purposes, in every case a licence to use the
drawings would necessarily be implied."*

The position was left uncertain. Now that the
RIBA Scale is no longer mandatory, the question
could become complicated unless the Standard
Form of Agreement for the Appointment of an
Architect (see page 30) is used, which makes
specific provisions with regard to copyright.
The Copyright Designs and Patents Act 1988 is
also relevant.

Recent Caselaw 2

3

MURPHY v. BRENTWOOD DISTRICT COUNCIL [1990] 50 BLR 1

- The Facts:
A housing estate was constructed in 1969 and the plaintiff bought one of a pair of semi-detached houses from the contractor in 1970. The concrete raft foundation design had been submitted to the Council. They had taken the advice of independent consulting engineers who recommended approval. The raft was subject to differential settlement causing cracking to the walls of the house and fracturing of a water pipe. The plaintiff was obliged to sell the house for considerably less than would have been its value if free from defects. The plaintiff brought an action for damages against the Council who were held liable to the plaintiff in negligence. An appeal to the Court of Appeal was dismissed and the Council appealed to the House of Lords.
- Held:
  - Negligence which results in a defect in the building itself is not actionable in tort.
  - In order to be actionable, the defect must cause damage to property other than the defective property or it must result in death or personal injury.
  - If the defect is discovered before it has caused any damage the cost of remedying the defect is not recoverable. There may be an exception if the defective structure is so close to the boundary as to pose a danger to other property after the defect is discovered.
  - It is not permissible to consider a complex structure such as a building as a complex structure in which one part caused damage to another, but there may be liability where a distinct item (e.g. a boiler) causes damage to the rest of the structure.
- Comment:
This is a very important case. It expressly overrules the decision in Anns v. Merton LBC [1978] 5 BLR 1 and any subsequent cases decided "in reliance on Anns". It takes further the principles set out in D & F Estates Ltd v. Church Commissioners [1988] 41 BLR 1 and effectively marks the end of actions in tort for the recovery of economic loss (except in the case of negligent mis-statement). The courts are laying increasing stress upon contracts and third party purchasers and tenants are finding themselves without adequate remedy for defects against consultants and builders. Hence the growth in demands for assignable collateral warranties to create contractual relationships where none would otherwise exist.

4

GREAVES & CO. (CONTRACTORS) LTD v BAYNHAM MEIKLE & PARTNERS [1974] 3 All ER 666

- The Facts:
The plaintiffs were builders who engaged the defendants as consultant engineers to design the structure of a warehouse required for the storing of full drums of oil which would be moved about on fork-lift stacker trucks. The design was executed in accordance with the relevant building regulations and codes of practice, the particularly relevant code of which contained a warning against structural damage which may be caused by vibrations set up by dynamic loads. The warehouse developed cracks, and the builders, who became liable to the owners, sought an indemnity from the defendant engineers. Expert evidence showed that the cracking was caused by random vibrations set up by the loaded trucks, of which the defendants had not taken sufficient account, having interpreted the code warning as referring only to repeated rhythmic impulses. Furthermore, a large number of professionals would have similarly interpreted the warning.
- Held:
Because the defendants ought to have been aware that the floor of the warehouse would carry heavily laden trucks, and since they had been warned of the dangers of vibration generally, the law imposed a higher duty on them than it did on professional men normally. It was their duty to ensure that the floor was fit for its intended purpose, and they were in breach of that duty.
- Comment:
The importance of this case lies in the fact that not only does a designer owe a general duty of care to his employer, but that contracts of this nature imply a term that the product should be fit for the purpose for which it is required. Care should therefore be taken to ensure that all available information as to proposed use is obtained prior to design.

5

SUTCLIFFE v THACKRAH & OTHERS [1974]
1 All ER 859

• The Facts:

The defendant architects were employed by the plaintiff to design a house. There was no formal contract, but the defendants knew that the JCT Standard Form of Contract was to be used. Under clause 30 of the 1963 Edition of the Standard Form, the architect was empowered to issue interim certificates at specified intervals. Subsequently the builders became insolvent and, finding the work to be defective, the plaintiff brought an action against the architects, alleging supervisory negligence, and negligence in issuing two interim certificates. The defendants claimed that they were acting in an arbitral capacity and, provided that they acted honestly, they were under no duty to exercise care or professional skill. The Court of Appeal agreed with them, but the plaintiff appealed to the House of Lords.

• Held:

An architect or valuer was generally liable to his employer if loss resulted from his negligence. However, immunity existed if the architect or valuer could show that, by agreement, he was appointed to act as an arbitrator or quasi-arbitrator to settle a specific dispute, and there was an agreement that his decision would be binding. The defendants had no immunity because (1) Issuing the interim certificate was not a decision resulting from a dispute.
(2) There was no agreement that the architect's decision would be binding in respect of the value of the work.
(3) The defendants owed the plaintiff a duty to exercise care and skill in issuing certificates.

• Comment:

This case clearly denies the architect's immunity in respect of certification under the JCT Form of Contract. Even if the architect's powers were derived from some other form of contract, no immunity would exist unless the three major points of the judgment were satisfied. Architects should now exercise extreme care before issuing any certificate.

6

PACIFIC ASSOCIATES INC & ANO v. BAXTER & OTHERS [1988] 44 BLR 33

• The facts:

The plaintiff entered into a contract with the employer to carry out dredging work in the Persian Gulf. The contract was on FIDIC Standard Form (1969 Edition). The plaintiff claimed that unexpected hard materials had been encountered, involving additional expense. The engineer refused to certify the claim for payment and the plaintiff started arbitration proceedings against the employer. The arbitration was settled and the plaintiff started proceedings on the same basis against the engineer alleging breach of a duty to use due care and to act impartially in certifying the payments which the plaintiff claimed as due in arbitration. The claim was rejected in the Official Referees Court and the plaintiff appealed.

• Held

-The engineer's obligations to use skill and care were owed contractually to the employer.
-The engineer did not assume liability to the contractor for economic loss arising out of breach of obligations in the FIDIC contract.
-There was no basis on which the engineer could be said to owe the contractor a duty of care.
-The engineer had a duty to the employer to act in accordance with the FIDIC contract. If the contractor wishes to challenge the engineer's performance, it should be done through the arbitration clause. There was no justification for imposing an additional liability in tort.

• Comment:

This case indicates that the courts are unwilling to open up a *tortious* route where a plaintiff has a remedy in contract for his damage. It can only be good news for the architect, but the courts are still some way from returning to the position in Bagot v. Stevens Scanlon & Co [1964] 3 All ER 577 that professional people owed duties only in contract. The principles in Pacific Associates have been followed in the recent Canadian case of Edgeworth Construction Ltd v. N D Lea & Associates Ltd [1991] 7 Const LJ 238. If the main contract, unusually, has no arbitration clause or the employer becomes insolvent, the position is less clear.

7

WHARF PROPERTIES LTD v. ERIC CUMINE ASSOCIATES [1991] 52 BLR 1

• The Facts:

The defendants were engaged as architects by the plaintiffs in connection with a large development in Hong Kong. The plaintiff claimed damages for negligence and breach of contract and commenced the action in 1983. Among other things, the plaintiff was attempting to recover from the defendant the amounts paid to other former defendants to reach a compromise. The statement of claim was a long document and the defendants sought an order that it should be struck out on the grounds that it disclosed no reasonable *cause* of action and it was an abuse of the process of the court. They stated that no link was shown between alleged breaches and the damages claimed. The High Court refused to strike out, but the Court of Appeal reversed the decision. The Plaintiffs appealed to the Privy Council of the House of Lords.

• Held:

The appeal should be dismissed. The *cause* of action was unreasonable although there would be great difficulties in proving the case. However, the claim should be struck out on the grounds that it was hopelessly embarrassing and constituted an abuse of the process of the court. The claim failed to specify any discernible connection between the alleged wrong and the consequent delay.

• Comments:

This case is about the importance of specifying the precise grounds of a claim and demonstrating the effect of each ground so as to clearly indicate to the defendant the case against him. The plaintiff tried to rely upon the decisions in J Crosby & Sons v. Portland UDC [1967] 5 BLR 121 and London Borough of Merton v. Stanley Hugh Leach Ltd [1985] 32 BLR 51 as authorities to support pleading the claim on a global basis. This was rejected. There are principles to be derived from this case which can be applied to the formulation and consideration of claims for loss and expense under the building contract, broadly; although there may be occasions when it is permissible to "roll up" the evaluation of a claim into a lump sum, it is never permissible to "roll up" the events and a clear link must be shown between each cause and its effect.

8

SMITH v. ERIC S BUSH and Harris v. WYRE FOREST DISTRICT COUNCIL [1989] 2 ER 514

• The Facts:

In the Smith case, the plaintiff applied for a mortgage. The building society instructed the defendants who were surveyors and valuers to value the property and note anything likely to affect its value. They failed to notice a defective chimney and gave a favourable report. The plaintiff bought the house relying solely on the report although she had been advised to get independent advice and the report contained a comprehensive disclaimer of liability. The chimney collapsed and the plaintiff claimed damages from the defendants in negligence. In the Harris case, the plaintiffs applied to the local Council for a loan for house purchase. The application form contained a disclaimer making clear that the valuation report was intended solely for the benefit of the Council which accepted no responsibility for the value or condition of the house. The Council advised the plaintiffs to obtain their own independent survey. They did not do so, but relied on the fact that they were offered a mortgage as indicative of the absence of serious faults. They proceeded with the purchase, but when they attempted to sell the house, serious faults became apparent and they brought an action in negligence against the Council and its agent. Both plaintiffs were successful at the first trial, but the Court of Appeal produced quite different results. An appeal was made to the House of Lords which considered both cases together.

• Held:

The valuer was liable in both cases. He knew that 90% of purchasers relied on the valuation and did not obtain independent reports. At common law a party was free to exclude liability for negligence, but the Unfair Contract Terms Act 1977 must be considered. S. 11(3) provided that regard should be had to all "circumstances obtaining when the liability arose or (but for the notice) was arisen" in deciding whether it would be fair and reasonable to allow reliance on a notice. The exclusion notices must satisfy the reasonableness test.

8 (continued)

Questions that should always be asked:
- Did the parties have equal bargaining power?
- Would it have been reasonably practicable for the purchaser to have obtained advice from another source?
- How difficult was the survey?
- What were the practical consequences?

Each case concerned a modest house and valuers knew the purchasers relied on their skill and care. In other situations, where large sums were at stake, the purchasers might be expected to commission independent surveys and the valuers might be considered to have acted reasonably in excluding or limiting their liability.

• Comment:

A milestone in the considerable case law on building surveys. The principles of liability are here relatively easily established on the basis of Hedley Byrne & Co Ltd v. Heller & Partners Ltd [1963]. The interest is in the exclusion clauses. It used to be standard practice to include a comprehensive disclaimer clause whenever a building survey was undertaken, because they were often carried out for relatively small fees in a short period of time and there is a substantial risk of overlooking a major defect in such instances. This case not only affects any architect who undertakes a building survey, but extends to all cases where a professional person gives any kind of service and attempts to modify liability by inserting an exclusion clause. It is clear that such attempted exclusions will be examined with great care by the Courts in the light of the Unfair Contract terms Act. Attempted total exclusions of liability will rarely, if ever succeed.

THE NEED FOR SAFEGUARDS

The law can be seen as a complex web of rules and procedures that either control or affect the actions of an individual or group. Transgression of the rules, whether intentional or otherwise, might lead to the implementation of prescribed punitive or compensatory measures by the controlling authorities.

In the field of construction, the potential problems arising from the intricacy of relationships and tasks, coupled with the ever-changing circumstances and conditions within which they are set, have led to the implementation of a number of precautions and remedies to either prevent or allow for certain contingencies. The most important of these are :

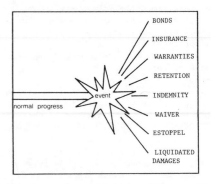

BONDS

Performance bonds fulfil a similar role to insurance where, for example, they may enable the employer to claim compensation for the underwriting surety in the event of non-completion by the contractor.

INSURANCE (see page 14)

Contracts of insurance may be entered into by the architect, the contractor, the sub-contractor and the employer to protect their respective interests. In the case of the contractor, this is compulsory (Standard Form cl.21)

WARRANTIES (see page 70)

Legally enforceable assurances given by parties in respect of their goods and services. They are contracts which run alongside and are collateral to another contract. They are often referred to as "collateral contracts". It is now usual for architects and other professionals to be asked for warranties (sometimes called "duty of care agreements") as a result of the difficulty in bringing actions in tort against architects following D & F Estates v. Church Commissioners [1988] and Murphy v. Brentwood [1990]. The warranties may be required in favour of the client, future tenants of the property, future purchasers or funding institutions. Model forms of warranty have been jointly developed by the British Property Federation, the Royal Institute of British Architects, the Royal Institution of Chartered Surveyors and the Association of Consulting Engineers. Use of these forms is not mandatory and a wide range of specially drafted warranties may be presented to the architect for signature. Some of the topics included in such warranties include:
• Standard of care.
• Consequential losses.
• Indemnity.
• Deleterious materials.
• Professional indemnity.
• Surrender of copyright.
• Assignment without consent.
• Extension of limitation period.
• Novation.

See Winwood Fearon, 'Collateral Warranties: a Practical Guide for the Construction Industry' 1990 Blackwell Scientific Publications Ltd, Oxford

RETENTION

At each stage of payment, an agreed percentage (which may vary from 3% on medium to large projects to 5% on small projects) will be retained by the employer. Half of this may be released upon the issuance of a Certificate of Practical Completion. Payment of the balance may depend upon the Completion of Making Good Defects or it may be retained until the Final Certificate, depending upon the form of contract in use. Recent case law has established that where the retention money is stated to be a trust fund (i.e. under JCT 80) the employer has an obligation to place it in a separate bank account even where the parties have deleted that stipulation from the contract.

Indemnity

An indemnity (or guarantee) is given by one party to secure another against loss or damage from specific liabilities (for example, Standard Form cl.20).

Waiver

A waiver indicates the relinquishing of specific rights by a party.

Estoppel

This is a doctrine which exists to prevent one party behaving inconsistently with his representation to another, in reliance of which the other has acted and suffered loss. In these circumstances, the first party could be 'estopped' from taking advantage of the situation by the Courts.

Liquidated Damages

These are damages which are agreed between the employer and the contractor (and stated in the Appendix). They provide a settled method of assessing damages arising out of late completion, (that is, £x per day or per week beyond the Date for Completion). The employer does not have to prove loss before he deducts the damages and he is entitled to deduct the amount stated (but no more) whether his loss is greater or less than the amount or even if he gains as a result of the delay. The amount stated must be a genuine pre-estimate by the employer of the loss he honestly believes he will suffer. The contractor may avoid paying liquidated damages:
• By obtaining an extension of time
• By showing that the Date for Completion no longer applies because the architect has failed to give an extension of time when one was due
• By showing that the amount started in the Appendix is legally a penalty (e.g. it is very much greater than could possibly represent a realistic pre-estimate of the likely amount).

Claims: Settle or Defend

If a complaint is made on the basis that legal obligations have not been fulfilled, the party so charged may admit responsibility and settle the claim by agreed damages, or other suitable means of compensation. Alternatively, he may refute the charge, in which case it is likely that the conflict will be dealt with by either LITIGATION (that is, through the civil courts) or ARBITRATION (that.

Shared Liability

It is possible in tort that parties may share the responsibility, in which case, they become JOINT TORTFEASORS in the same action.

Time Limits

Lapse of time may afford protection to a negligent party. The Limitation Acts 1939 & 1980 set down time limits in respect of certain types of action, notably:

6 years in respect of a contract under hand (i.e. just signed by the parties).
12 years in respect of a contract entered into as a deed.

Beyond these periods, no action may be taken.

The Latent Damage Act 1986 lays down time limits in respect of negligent actions involving property. They are either:
• 6 years from the day the cause of the action arose
or
• 3 years from the date the plaintiff acquired knowledge of the damage and the identity of the defendant, if this period expires later than the six years noted above.
• In any case, a longstop period of 15 years from the date of the negligent action applies, after which no action can be brought.

R
E   LAW MADE SIMPLE. pp.128, 146, 178, 208,
F   246-247.

Insurance

A contract of insurance arises when one party undertakes to make payments for the benefit of another in the event of certain events taking place. The conditions upon which such a payment would occur are usually described in detail in the POLICY.

The CONSIDERATION (see page 54) necessary to validate the contract is called the PREMIUM, and insurance cover is often secured through a BROKER. Many architects utilise the services offered by:

RIBA Insurance Agency
53 Eastcheap
London
EC3P 3HL

Types

There are two kinds of insurance:

- INDEMNITY INSURANCE.
  This ensures the payment of compensation for losses incurred by certain events, e.g. fire, motor safety or third party liability.
- NON-INDEMNITY INSURANCE.
  In this case a specific sum is paid on the occurrence of a specified event, e.g. attainment of a certain age.

Contracts of insurance are said to be 'of the utmost good faith' (*uberrimae fidei*). This means that all material facts must be disclosed to the insurer which might affect his willingness to accept the risk. Failure to disclose may render the contract voidable. Indemnity insurance should be considered in three categories:

PROFESSIONAL INDEMNITY
SITE INSURANCE
LATENT DEFECTS INSURANCE

Professional Indemnity

Professional indemnity insurance is a precautionary measure often taken to protect the architect, his partners and employees from claims arising from their negligent acts. Care should be taken to ensure that each new partner or employee is covered under the terms of the policy, and that any unusual features of the office (involvement in overseas work, for example) are covered.

Coverage

Coverage of indemnity insurance may include:

- PROFESSIONAL NEGLIGENCE
- INFRINGEMENT OF COPYRIGHT
- LOSS OF DOCUMENTS
- RECOVERY OF PROFESSIONAL FEES
- DISHONESTY OF EMPLOYEES
- DEFAMATION

Continuing coverage on withdrawal or retirement by a member should be carefully considered in the light of recent caselaw.

Site Insurance

The contractor is responsible for taking control of the site, and must maintain insurances to cover his liability (and that of his sub-contractors) in respect of personal injury (JCT Standard Form of Contract 1980, CL. 21.1.1.1). He must also insure against damage to the property arising from his actions.

The architect has the right (cl.21.1.2) to inspect the contractor's insurance in respect of the site, and should the latter default, the employer may insure and deduct the cost of the premium from the contractor's fees.

The site must also be insured against damage by fire and other accidents in the joint names of the employer and contractor.

Adjustments to the site insurance should be made:
- ON SECTIONAL COMPLETION, if appropriate
- ON PRACTICAL COMPLETION
- ON FINAL COMPLETION
- IN THE EVENT OF ANY MATERIAL CHANGE THAT MAY AFFECT THE POLICY

Latent Defects Insurance

This is sometimes known as BUILD (Building Users Insurance Against Latent Defects). It is a non-cancellable insurance against major latent defects for a fixed period (usually 10 years) involving payment of a single premium by the building owner and it is assignable to future owners of the building.

FURTHER COVERAGE

It is also advisable to consider the need for insuring against:

- EMPLOYER'S LIABILITY, covering the death or injury of employees under the Employees Liability (Compulsory Insurance) Act 1969.
- PUBLIC LIABILITY, to cover third parties.
- BUILDING AND CONTENTS, either on an indemnity or reinstatement basis.
- MOTOR CARS, if used for business purposes.

It may also be worthwhile considering insurance in respect of:

TRAVEL HAZARDS
STAFF WELFARE
PENSIONS

Points to Remember

- Keep all policies safely at the principal place of business.
- Notify insurers of all matters which may affect the risk ('good faith' principle)
- Ensure that renewal dates are noted in order that premiums can be promptly paid
- Check all policies periodically to ensure that the amount of cover is adequate.
- Consider the benefit of index-linked policies.
- Notify insurers of all new staff relevant to the Professional Indemnity Policy.

- Never take insurance cover for granted. If in doubt as to whether a risk is covered, check with the insurers first.

R E F

PRACTICE MANAGEMENT HANDBOOK. pp. 56-57, 79-81, 171
THE ARCHITECT'S GUIDE TO RUNNING A JOB. pp. 76-77.
ARCHITECT'S LEGAL HANDBOOK. pp. 42-43, 278-82.

MEMO

To   : Tom
From   : Bill
Date   : 5th Jan
Concerning : Unpaid fees

Tom — have been looking
through outstanding a/c's
& note that your Mr Fox
hasn't settled the final
account we sent to
him 6 months ago.
Please could you
deal with this ASAP.

JUSTIN CASE

Insurance
Broker

5.JAN.94

Dear Sirs,

re: Policy No.163468 - Fire Insurance.

I note from our records that the premium in respect
of your above-numbered policy is due on the 14th
of this month. I would draw you attention to the
availability of index-linked policies, which lessen
the need to constantly reassess the amount of
cover necessary. If you would be interested in
discussing a transfer to this type of policy,
please telephone me to arrange an appointment.

Yours faithfully,

J. Case.

J.Case.

10, Tative Approach, Cringing, Wilts

LOCKE, STOCKE and BARRELL.

A.Locke.LLB(Lond).
J.Stocke.MA(Oxon).   SOLICITORS
B.Barrell.BA(Rangoon).

Our Ref: AL/gy
Your Ref:

1, Fore Hall,
Cringing,
Wilts.

Dear Sirs,   15.1.94

WITHOUT PREJUDICE.

re: A Payne Esq.

We have been consulted by your above-named ex-employee who informs us
that he suffered an injury while preparing drawings in the course of
his employment.

We understand that Mr Payne fell from a faulty stool and impaled the third
finger of his right hand on a drawing pen nib. In consequence, Mr Payne
has lost much of the sensitivity in this finger and, being a keen bowls
enthusiast is now deprived of his major pastime.

We have advised our client that he has a good case in tort, since the
accident resulted from your firm's negligence. However, our client is
disposed to settle this matter for a payment of £900.

We look forward to receiving your comments,

Yours faithfully,

Locke Stocke
& Barrell

Locke, Stocke and Barrell.

Fair and Square,
ellovet,

DESK DIARY

JAN 19

Re: Fox, outstanding fees.
Check today to see if he pays up, following our letter.
If not, discuss with Bill whether or not to sue.
Is it worth it for this amount? The costs involved may
not make it worthwhile. Might consider another letter
from solicitors or a small claims action though.

JAN 20

Re: Payne's finger.
- Have acknowledged receipt of letter from L.S.B,
but haven't commented.
- Have informed our solicitors & insurers —
sounds like a try-on, but you never know —
I didn't know Arthur played bowls!

MEMO

To : Tom
From : Bill
Date. : 7th Jan
Concerning : Insurance renewal

Do we need to increase cover re
increased property value & new
office equipment? If so, by how much? we
Motor premiums also due soon — we
must insure RoyTing's Mini, as he's
using it for site visits, and may not
covered on his domestic policy.
...or suggests index-linked
...es — sounds good.

Fair and Square

CHARTERED ARCHITECTS

B.FAIR.dip.arch.RIBA.
T.SQUARE.B.Arch.RIBA.AFAS.

Our Ref: TS/vn

4, The Hell
Cringing,
Wilts.

Dear Mr Fox,

Jan.6th.94

re: Outstanding fees for house extension at
Witt's End.

Further to our letters of the 23rd Sept. and the 3rd Dec.1982,
we note that your final account is still outstanding to the
sum of £780.

We regret to inform you that if payment in full is not
received within 14 days of the date of this letter, we shall
be compelled to institute proceedings against you in the
County Court.

We look forward to hearing from you,

Yours sincerely,

Fair & Square.

Fair and Square.

A.Fox Esq.
Taxfrey Haven,
Cringing,
Wilts.

SECTION TWO

THE BUILDING INDUSTRY

Contents   Page

Relationships
within the
Building Industry

Forms of Association 1

Parties operating within the construction industry have different legal personalities according to the type of association to which they belong. This personality affects the relationship between the law, the employer and the individual. Major methods of operating a business are :

1. Single Individual

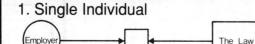

This is the simplest form of association, where the responsibilities and liabilities are clearly defined e.g. a sole practitioner of architecture or a builder

2. Partnership

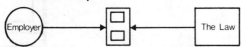

A partnership exists where two or more individuals carry on a business in common with a view to profit, the profit to be shared in the proportions agreed by the partners. In general, partnership is governed by the provisions of the Partnership Act 1890, and it is a common method of practising architecture as it enables the parties to share their expertise, capital and resources.

The formation of a partnership does not limit the responsibility of the individuals involved, and partners remain personally liable for all negligent acts of the firm. However, the partnership may sue or be sued in the name of partnership.

Formation

The partnership relationship can be created by:
- CONDUCT OF THE PARTIES
- ORAL AGREEMENT
- WRITTEN AGREEMENT

The latter is by far the most satisfactory, where all terms, conditions and implications of the relationship can be fully explored before a binding agreement is made.

Types of Practitioner

a THE EQUITY PARTNER
This is a full partnership arrangement, where the partner enjoys the full benefits and responsibilities of the firm.

b THE SALARIED PARTNER
A salaried partnership is in effect a 'name only' arrangement, enabling the recipient to have his name on the letterhead of the firm. However, the implication may be that he shares the same liabilities as the equity partners, and an indemnity should be obtained from the equity partners in respect of partnership liabilities and debts. Before accepting a salaried partnership, it should be remembered that all rights of redundancy pay and unfair dismissal compensation would be lost, and that the income tax position may also be affected. However, a salaried partnership may have advantages in the form of a share of the profits or as an interim step before final commitment to the firm.

c THE LIMITED PARTNER
The Limited Partnership Act 1907 provides for this type of partner, whose liability is limited to the extent of his capital investment. Such a partner does not usually become involved in the management of the firm.

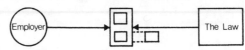

d THE ASSOCIATE
Although a salaried position, an associateship indicates a certain status, and may carry a small share in the firm's profits.
There can be uncertainty as to the liability of the position in relation to the partners, and, as with salaried partners, the extent of the responsibilities and liabilities of the associate should be clearly stated in the agreement or letter of acceptance. The position should also be made clear in the associate's dealings with the public so as to avoid the possible assumption of his equality with the partners. (for example, letterheads should be clearly marked with the associate's name and position, preferably distinct from those of the partners).

e THE DIRECTOR
The architect can carry on business as a director of a limited company (see page 19), subject to professional indemnity insurance provisions.

Termination

The partnership agreement can be terminated by:
- EXPIRATION of an agreed time period.
- COMPLETION of a designated task or project.
- DEATH of one of the partners.
- BANKRUPTCY of a partner.
- RETIREMENT of a partner.
- MUTUAL AGREEMENT.
- BY ORDER OF THE COURT.
- BY SUBSEQUENT ILLEGALITY.

In some cases, it is desirable to include provisions in the partnership agreement to enable the firm to continue despite certain of the above events happening. e.g. death

Title and Tax

a Since the Companies Act 1981, it is unnecessary to register the firm name and the names of all the partners, but if the word 'architect' is used in the firm name, ARCUK's approval is needed.

b Partners are liable to income tax under Schedule D, but not to corporation tax. However, they should ensure that a tax reserve is maintained to satisfy their annual obligations.

Partnership Checklist

- Names, signatures and date of agreement.
- Dates or time of termination (if any).
- Name of firm and address of business location.
- Contribution of capital and provisions for withdrawal.
- Division of partners' time, liabilities, responsibilities and duties.
- Salaries and profit-sharing procedures.
- Methods of accounting, investments and banking.
- Insurances, including provisions for ongoing coverage of outgoing partner.
- Rights of all partners in death sickness, retirement and withdrawal of a partner.
- Arbitration agreement.
- Length of holidays.
- Provisions for cheque-writing, hiring and firing.
- Property of partners loaned to firm.
- Provisions in case of disqualification, bankruptcy or misconduct of a partner.
- Restraint of trade covenants (if any)
- General provisions for dissolution.
- Pensions for outgoing partners or their widows.

3. Limited Companies

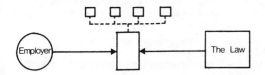

A limited company is a form of corporation limited in liability to the amount of shares or guarantee. It exists as a separate legal entity distinct from its shareholders, whose personal wealth is immune from claims made against the company. The assets of a limited company are contributed by its members, who buy shares representing the limit of their responsibility in the company.

Types

There are two kinds of limited company:

PUBLIC
PRIVATE

- PUBLIC LIMITED COMPANIES
These have unlimited membership and have their shares quoted on the Stock Exchange. The shares are freely transferable.
- PRIVATE LIMITED COMPANIES
These are usually smaller, and while there is no limitation on the number of members, if membership falls below two for six months, personal liability can be incurred. The shares are not freely transferable.

Formation

The formation of a limited company requires:

- ARTICLES OF ASSOCIATION
- MEMORANDUM OF AGREEMENT

ARTICLES regulate the management and procedures that the company will follow, while THE MEMORANDUM OF ASSOCIATION sets out the objectives of the company. (In the case of a public company, this is dealt with in the Charter or Statute which created it). The powers of the company thus stated must not be exceeded, otherwise the company acts *ultra vires* (beyond its powers).

4. Unlimited Companies

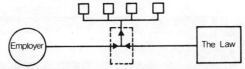

These are fairly unusual forms of corporations, as the shareholders do not have their liability limited to the value of their shares. Advantages of this form of association may include the achievement of corporate status and certain legal and tax benefits.

5. Group Practice

This is useful form of association often found in the practice of architecture, where the advantages may include:
- SHARED RESOURCES
- SHARED CAPITAL
- SHARED EXPERTISE and KNOWLEDGE
- FLUIDITY OF STAFF ALLOCATION

There are five types of group practice:

1 THE GROUP ASSOCIATION
This is a loose arrangement of architectural firms, pooling knowledge and experience but retaining their individual identities in their dealings with employers.

2 SHARED FACILITIES
Several firms may share facilities and operate either singly or in unison.

3 GROUP COORDINATING FIRM
Here, elements of a master plan are delegated to separate firms and coordinated by the architect responsible for the initial production of the master plan. He also remains answerable to the employer.

4 SINGLE PROJECT GROUP PARTNERSHIP
The partnership exists for a specified time, or for a specified purpose only, at the end of which it automatically dissolves.

5 GROUP PARTNERSHIP
Where firms retain their individual identities, but combine together in a continuing relationship for certain projects.

Other Forms

Other forms of association connected with parties involved in the construction industry include:

A TRADE UNIONS
B LOCAL AUTHORITIES
C THE CROWN
D PUBLIC CORPORATIONS

A TRADE UNIONS
These are groups formed within the trades with the objective of collectively bargaining for pay and conditions of employment.

B LOCAL AUTHORITIES
These are corporate bodies whose constitution and powers are derived from statutes. Their contractual powers are similar to those of an incorporated company, where the council is vicariously responsible for its employees. (Professional employees, however, may have a personal liability in tort regardless of this relationship).
The authorities are composed of metropolitan, county and district councils, each consisting of elected aldermen and councillors.

C THE CROWN
This title refers to all governmental powers expressed through the Civil Service at central government level. (It also refers to the Rights and immunities of the reigning monarch). Since 1947, a government department may be sued through the ordinary courts.

D PUBLIC CORPORATIONS
These are concerned with the nationalised industries, and were created by statute to be operated by the State. Their contractual powers are essentially the same as incorporated companies (that is, they may not operate *ultra vires*).

R
E
F

LAW MADE SIMPLE. pp. 100-107.
ARCHITECT'S LEGAL HANDBOOK. pp. 268-79
PM HANDBOOK. pp. 111-130.
THE ARCHITECT IN PRACTICE. pp. 40-51.
RIBA 'GUIDE TO GROUP PRACTICE & CONSORTIA'.

The Building Process - Parties Involved

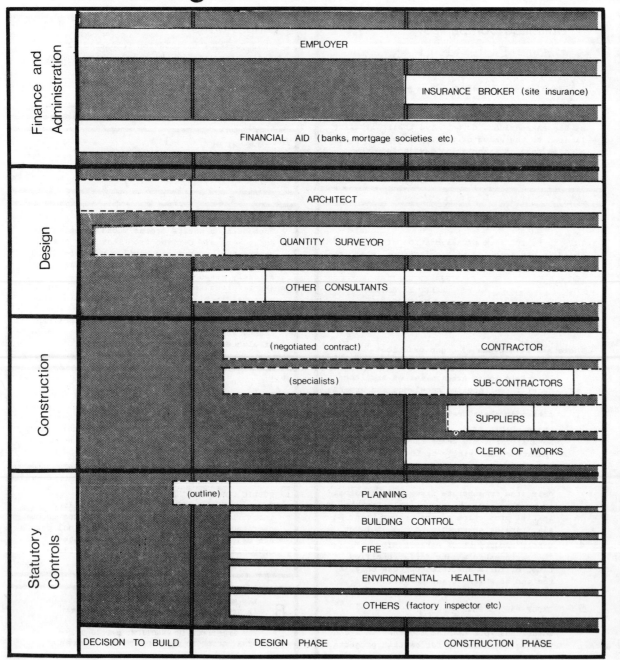

	DECISION TO BUILD	DESIGN PHASE	CONSTRUCTION PHASE
Finance and Administration	EMPLOYER		
			INSURANCE BROKER (site insurance)
	FINANCIAL AID (banks, mortgage societies etc)		
Design	ARCHITECT		
	QUANTITY SURVEYOR		
		OTHER CONSULTANTS	
Construction		(negotiated contract)	CONTRACTOR
		(specialists)	SUB-CONTRACTORS
			SUPPLIERS
			CLERK OF WORKS
Statutory Controls	(outline)	PLANNING	
		BUILDING CONTROL	
		FIRE	
		ENVIRONMENTAL HEALTH	
		OTHERS (factory inspector etc)	

Related Organisations

Professional institutes and associations (trade, standards and research) within the building industry include:

ARBITRATORS, CHARTERED INSTITUTE OF
ACOUSTICS, INSTITUTE OF
ADVISORY CONCILIATION AND ARBITRATION SERVICE
AGRÉMENT BOARD
ARCHITECTS AND SURVEYORS, INSTITUTE OF
ARCHITECTS AND SURVEYORS, INCORPORATED
                    ASSOCIATION OF
ARCHITECT'S REGISTRATION COUNCIL OF
                    THE UNITED KINGDOM
BRITISH INSTITUTE OF ARCHITECTURAL TECHNICIANS
BRITISH STANDARDS INSTITUTION
BUILDERS MERCHANTS FEDERATION
BUILDERS, INSTITUTE OF
BUILDING COMPONENTS MANUFACTURERS, ASSOC. OF
BUILDING CONTROL OFFICERS, INSTITUTION OF
BUILDING, CHARTERED INSTITUTE OF
BUILDING MATERIALS PRODUCERS, NATIONAL COUNCIL
BUILDING RESEARCH ADVISORY COUNCIL
BUILDING RESEARCH ESTABLISHMENT
BUILDING SERVICES, CHARTERED INSTITUTION OF
BUILDING SERVICES RESEARCH AND INFORMATION
                    ASSOCIATION
BUILDING SUB-CONTRACTORS, FEDERATION OF
CHARTERED SURVEYORS, ROYAL INSTITUTION OF
CIVIL ENGINEERING CONTRACTORS, FEDERATION OF
CIVIL ENGINEERS, INSTITUTION OF
CLERK OF WORKS OF GREAT BRITAIN, INSTITUTE OF
CONSTRUCTION INDUSTRY RESEARCH AND INFORMATION
                    ASSOCIATION
ELECTRICAL ENGINEERS, INSTITUTION OF
FIRE OFFICERS COMMITTEE
FIRE PROTECTION ASSOCIATION
HEATING AND VENTILATION CONTRACTORS ASSOCIATION
HEATING AND VENTILATION ENGINEERS, INSTITUTE OF
HOUSE BUILDING COUNCIL, NATIONAL
JOINT CONTRACTS TRIBUNAL
LANDSCAPE INSTITUTE
MASTER BUILDERS, FEDERATION OF
MECHANICAL ENGINEERS, INSTITUTION OF
NATIONAL BUILDING AGENCY
NATIONAL BUILDING SPECIFICATIONS SERVICES
PLUMBING, INSTITUTE OF
ROYAL INSTITUTE OF BRITISH ARCHITECTS
SALARIED ARCHITECTS GROUP
STRUCTURAL ENGINEERS, INSTITUTION OF
TOWN PLANNING INSTITUTE, ROYAL
Addresses or organisations which may be of most use to the architect are included on pages 101 and 102

The Architect/Employer

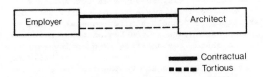

━━━━ Contractual
▪▪▪▪ Tortious

The relationship between the architect and his employer is primarily contractual, and as such is governed by the terms of the contract between them. The contract invariably formalises a relationship of AGENCY, where the architect (the agent) acts as the employer's representative, working solely in the latter's best interests.
AGENCY may be : UNIVERSAL, where for example, there is a power of attorney.
GENERAL, within a defined area of duty (for example, a solicitor).
SPECIAL, where the contract involved is for a specified purpose (such as the design and supervision of a construction project). This type of agency is nearly always detailed in a written agreement.

An agent is expected to work with the level of skill normally associated with his profession or occupation, and be concerned not to allow a conflict to arise between his own interests and those of his principal. The agency authority of the architect is limited to the terms of the appointment, and he has no authority, for example, to vary the contract between the contractor and employer unless express powers are granted for such a purpose.

The architect's contract with the employer is one 'for services' rather than a contract 'of service'. This distinction depends on the degree of control exercised by the employer, and affects his vicarious liability in tort. The general rule holds an employer vicariously liable for acts of those employed under a contract of service. (see p. 33 for Employer Profile).

The Architect/Consultant

Where services necessary to a construction project are outside the normal services offered by the architect, specialists may be employed directly by the employer on advice from the architect. This separation of the roles of architect and consultant prevents any possibility of claims for vicarious responsibility between the two.

The following areas are outside normal architectural services:

- QUANTITY SURVEYING (see p.22)
- TOWN PLANNING
- CIVIL ENGINEERING
- STRUCTURAL ENGINEERING
- MECHANICAL ENGINEERING
- ELECTRICAL ENGINEERING
- INDUSTRIAL DESIGN
- INTERIOR DESIGN
- LANDSCAPE AND GARDEN DESIGN
- FURNITURE DESIGN
- GRAPHIC DESIGN

More care must be taken when the architect wishes the employer to contract with a consultant for work within the architect's normal services which he wishes to delegate due to time, staff shortages etc. In such circumstances, the consultant's responsibilities and liabilities should be carefully detailed in the agreement to avoid any confusion in the event of loss or damage. Furthermore, the hiring of such a consultant may justify a reduction in the architect's fees.
Whatever arrangements are eventually made, the employer should be made aware as early as possible of the necessity and implications of hiring consultants.

The Architect/Contractor

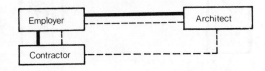

There is no contractual connection between these parties, as the contractor is directly responsible to the employer under the building contract. However, most contracts for construction contain provisions enabling the architect to fulfil certain prescribed duties in the capacity of agent (Standard Form clauses 2 and 4).

Errors made by the architect which cause loss to the contractor could not lead to an action in contract (see page 54), but could form the basis for a claim against the employer. This may in turn lead to an action by the employer against the architect for breach of the contract between them.
Alternatively, the contractor could sue the architect in tort, where no contractual connection is necessary but the chances of recovering damages are slight.
The same situation arises between the architect and the sub-contractors (whose contract will be with the contractor or employer), and the suppliers (who will deal directly with the contractors and sub-contractors).

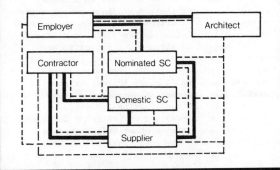

R
E
F

PRACTICE MANAGEMENT HANDBOOK. pp. 192-198
ARCHITECT'S LEGAL HANDBOOK. p. 5.
THE ARCHITECT IN PRACTICE. pp. 67-99

The Quantity Surveyor

Appointment

On most larger construction projects, a quantity surveyor would be instructed, essentially for the purpose of preparing bills of quantities and generally controlling cost throughout the building stages.

At what level of construction the employment of a quantity surveyor becomes viable depends on the nature of the work. Should the employer be reluctant to make an appointment though, it may be necessary to point out that the work needed falls outside the normal architectural services and, if undertaken by the architect, will merit additional fees.

R.I.C.S.

The Chartered Quantity Surveyor is a member of the Royal Institution of Chartered Surveyors, a respected professional body which comments on proposed legislation in the field of management, valuation and development of property, and planning provisions. It also aims to ensure high academic and professional standards in its members, and, among other things, it provides a useful cost information service for those involved in the construction industry.
The RICS is represented on the Joint Contracts Tribunal, and on most other British bodies associated with the construction industry.

The quantity surveyor might be described as a 'building economist', and as such he plays an important part in the construction process.

Normal Services

Normal services offered by the quantity surveyor include:

- Cost advice on the proposed scheme.
- Advice on the economics of the project, and preparation of a budget.
- Given a fixed cost, advice on size and structure.
- Advice on cost feasibility at the outline and scheme design stages.
- Cost assessment of detailed design and production drawings against the cost plan.
- Advice on tendering and type of contract suitable for the project.
- Preparation of documents for arranging tenders and the building contract.
- Preparation of Bills of Quantities.
- Examination of tenders.
- Ongoing check on the cost plan throughout the construction phase.
- Valuations for interim certificates.
- Preparation of the final account, including adjustment of the contract sum for variations and claims for delay.
- Advice on the financial implications of unplanned actions during construction (for example, variations).

Additional Services

Additional services of the quantity surveyor might include:

- Cost in use studies involving discounted cash flow techniques.
- Valuation of reports (structural, schedules of defects, etc.).
- Advice on capital investment policy, and cost implications of site selection.
- Advice on comparative costs of specialised building types and on performance specifications.
- Life cycle cost analysis.

Preliminary Advice

Even if a quantity surveyor is not appointed for a project, it may still be useful for the architect to consult him for general advice on approximate costs at the beginning of a scheme, at the sketch design stage. A quantity surveyor is able to judge the size and type of building feasible having regard to the finance available, and may thus safe the architect a great deal of unnecessary work.

The employer usually contracts directly with the quantity surveyor, using the standard form produced by the Royal Institution of Chartered Surveyors for this purpose.
Fee Scales are recommended and fee tendering is possible.

Other Surveyors

Members of the Royal Institution of Chartered Surveyors practice in a number of fields other than quantity surveying:

- Agricultural Surveying
- Auctioneering
- Building Surveying
- Estate Agency
- Forestry Management
- Hydrographic Surveying
- Housing Management
- Land Agency
- Land Economy
- Land Surveying
- Town Planning
- Urban Estate Management
- Valuation Surveying
- Mining Surveying
- Mineral Surveying

In addition, THE CONTRACTOR'S SURVEYOR is a full-time employee of the contractor whose role is more that of a building accountant than building economist. He is responsible for submitting interim valuations, agreeing rates for variations, administration of sub-contracts, preparation of claim submissions and agreement of the final account.

R
E
F

PRACTICE MANAGEMENT HANDBOOK. pp. 195.
THE ARCHITECT IN PRACTICE. pp. 5-7.
RICS: 'THE CHARTERED QUANTITY SURVEYOR : THE EXPERT IN CONSTRUCTION VALUES'.

1, Thewist Drive,
Cringing,
Wilts

February 11th.

Dear Mr Square,
    I am still not happy about the expense involved
in appointing a quantity surveyor as you suggested at our
last meeting. I always understood that such matters could be
dealt with by the architect. Unless you can assure me
otherwise, I would rather not be put to this added expense.

    Yours sincerely,

    B. Careful

B. Careful

MEMO

To   Tom
From   Bill
Date   16th Feb.
Concerning R. Tring — Associateship

Roy informs me that he's keen on our
proposal to make him an associate on
the terms mentioned, but he's rather
concerned about his position with
regard to his personal liability
Can we clarify the position for him?

Tom,
    We're a bit pushed for time
on the factory job — why
don't we push out the
tendering work to a consultant?
Could you suggest someone?

    Bill

23

DESK DIARY

FEB 17

Re: Roy's Associateship.
Must contact our insurers & inform them of the
new position.

FEB 18

BILL - GOT YOUR MEMO ABOUT ROY'S ASSOCIATESHIP. SUGGEST THE FOLLOWING
POINTS SHOULD BE COVERED IN A LETTER OF CONFIRMATION TO KEEP
THE RECORDS STRAIGHT:
1   DETAILS OF SALARY
2   DETAILS OF PROFIT SHARING
3   CAREFUL DEFINITION OF RESPONSIBILITIES
    OF THE PARTNERSHIP (REMEMBER INSURANCES).
4   REQUIREMENT OF CONTINUING RIBA MEMBERSHIP
5   CLEAR DEFINITION OF THE ASSOCIATE STATUS
    ON LETTER-HEAD AND IN OUR BROCHURE

Tom.

MEMO

To   : Bill

From   : Tom

Date   : 18th Feb.

Concerning : subbing out work. - Careful!

This phase is part of basic services - if someone else is
employed we have to reduce our fees. If we employ someone
~~~ responsibilities/liabilities start getting complex.
~~~ did it we ask Roy to take a look at it?
                                                    T.

Fair and Square

B.FAIR.dip.arch.RIBA.   CHARTERED   ARCHITECTS
T.SQUARE.B.Arch.RIBA.AFAS.

TS/vn

4, The He
Cringing,
Wilts.

Dear Mr Careful,

                                                    12.2.94

                re: Proposed development at Cheapsgate, Cringing.

Thank you for your letter of the 11th Feb, expressing concern
in respect of appointing a quantity surveyor on the above
project. We appreciate your desire to keep costs at a minimum,
but are of the opinion that a quantity surveyor would make a
valuable contribution to the scheme for the following reasons:

1. A quantity surveyor specialises in building
economics, and is therefore able to provide you
with expert advice regarding structure, materials,
methods of construction etc. most appropriate and
economically viable for your particular project.
2. A quantity surveyor is also a building accountant,
and can not only plan and check costs before and
during the project, but will prepare Bills of
Quantities, periodical and final valuations and
advice on proposed or necessary variations that may
occur.
3. Although architects can deal with measurement and
valuation, work in this field falls outside the
Architect's Normal Services (as stated in your copy of
the Standard Form of Agreement for the Appointment of
an Architect), and extra fees for this work would become
chargeable under Schedule Two.

I hope the points raised in this letter adequately satisfy
your doubts, and we look forward to receiving your instructions
regarding the appointment of a quantity surveyor in due course.

                    Yours sincerely,

                    Fair & Square.
                    Fair and Square.

SECTION THREE

THE ARCHITECT IN PRACTICE

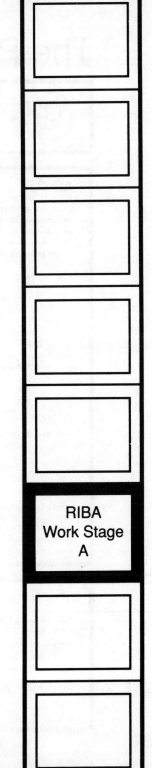

RIBA
Work Stage
A

The Profession 1

ARCUK

This is governed by the Architects' Registration Acts 1931-1969, which provide that all suitably qualified persons must be registered with ARCUK if they wish to practise under the title of 'architect'.

The three principal objectives of ARCUK are:
- To maintain a register of architects.
- To monitor and uphold professional conduct.
- To award scholarships to needy students.

Membership of ARCUK may be attained:
- By passing prescribed examinations.
- By being a member of the Royal Academy or the Royal Scottish Academy.
- By qualifications prescribed by Privy Council approved regulations.

Removal from the register may result from:
- Non-payment of fees.
- Non-notification of change of address.
- Criminal offences or disgraceful conduct in regard to the practice of architecture.

Several professional bodies are represented in ARCUK, including the Royal Institute of British Architects, the Architects and Surveyors Institute and the Incorporated Association of Architects and Surveyors.

The RIBA

The major professional organisation for architects was founded in 1834 and is located in Portland Place. Its objects are:
- To promote the highest standards of architecture.
- To conserve and improve the architectural environment.
- To provide a single voice for the profession as a whole.

Membership

The RIBA has two types of membership:
- CORPORATE
- NON-CORPORATE

There is one class of corporate member, who can use the title 'chartered architect' and the affix RIBA if he is on the ARCUK register and has paid his membership fees;

Non-corporate membership is secured in three ways:
- By subscription of registered architects (Subscribers).
- By subscription of students from recognised institutions (Student Members).
- By appointment to Honorary Fellow, or Corresponding Member if outside the United Kingdom (Honorary Members).

Structure

The council of the RIBA is the governing body of the Institute and is headed by the President. It comprises the immediate past President, a past President, Vice Presidents and nationally and regionally elected members. The work of the Council is co-ordinated by the Co-ordinating Committee which is chaired by the President. The RIBA carries out a number of functions, which are grouped under 6 standing committees and 2 committees (Professional Conduct and Disciplinary Committees) which, although not standing committees, report directly to the Council:

1 Practice Committee

Responsible for considering matters and issuing directions regarding aspects of professional practice including:
- Preparation and advice on Architect's conditions of engagement and fees.
- Promoting the use and continued improvement of the Standard Form of Building Contract (through the Joint Contracts Tribunal).
- Development of standards for the construction industry
- Monitoring and advising on the development of building control.
- Liaison with BIAT to consider standards of technical education.
- Promoting the establishment of clear guidelines on professional liability through (among other things) submissions to the Law Reform Committee.

- Formulation of the Code of Professional Conduct.
- Liaison with the Architects' Benevolent Society.
- Research into the problems of inner cities.
- Promotion of community architecture.
- Initiatives by the Community Urban Development Team (CUDAT) in specific areas of the country.
- Promotion of initiatives on energy management.

2 Resource, Planning and Finance Committee

Responsible for:
- Institute's long and short term financial affairs.
- The budget.
- Financial business, investment and borrowing of funds.

It also provides accounting services for the RIBA subsidiary companies:
- RIBA Services Ltd/Library Planning Consultants Ltd.
  Handles technical and advisory services to the profession and the building industry;producing product data, office library services and developing the CI/Sfb system of classification.
- RIBA Publications Ltd. Produces a wide range of publications, contract documents and ancilliary materials, on sale at RIBA Bookshops throughout the country.
- RIBA Magazines Ltd.
  Produces the RIBA Journal.
- NBS Services Ltd.
  An extensive catalogue of specification clauses in standard form.

3 Education and Professional Development Committee

Responsible for:
- Policy proposals on education and CPD.
- Monitoring trends in education.
- Examination and qualification arrangements.
- Relations with schools of architecture.
- Maintenance of agreed regulatory framework.
- Liaison with government and other bodies on educational matters.
- Furtherance of all aspects of architectural education, including promoting public awareness and the understanding of architecture and the built enviroment in primary and secondary schools.

4 Marketing Committee

Responsible for the promotional aspects of the Institute's work, including:
- Presenting architects and architecture to the public.
- Identification of future markets for the profession.
- Generation of funding.
- Helping to ensure that architects offer the appropriate standards of service.
- The making of awards for outstanding buildings.
- Through the Client's Advisory Service, giving advice to members of the public on the selection of an architect.
- Parliamentary lobbying.
- Corporate publicity for the profession.

5 Library Committee

Responsible for:
- Advising on the maintenance and development of the collection.
- Advising on the development of appropriate policies.
- Library accommodation.
- Books, periodicals and drawings.
- Mounting exhibitions.
- Loans to exhibitions.
- Special publications.
- Advising (through the Professional Literature Committee) authors and publishers.
- Publishing the RIBA book list.

6 Membership Committee

Responsible for:
- Internal administration and management of the Institute.
- Financing the regions.
- Review of the membership structure.
- Salaries Architects Group.

Also responsible for monitoring the work of the International Affairs Committee:
- Representation in Commonwealth Association of Architects (CAA).
- Representation in the International Union of Architects (UIA).
- Representation in the Architects Council of Europe (ACE).
- Maintaining relations with individual professional bodies in Europe.
- Nominating architects for study tours as part of the UK Cultural Exchange Agreements.
- Advising practices who wish to work overseas.

7. PROFESSIONAL CONDUCT COMMITTEE

Advises members on questions of conduct, investigates suspected beaches of the Code of Professional Conduct and formulates charges, in serious cases, for determination by the Disciplinary Committee.

8 DISCIPLINARY COMMITTEE

Hears evidence and has the power to order suspension or expulsion of members, if appropriate.

R
E
F
PRACTICE MANAGEMENT HANDBOOK.pp.11-24
THE ARCHITECT IN PRACTICE.p.17-22

The Office

Setting Up

There a number of legal obligations that must be taken into consideration when setting up and running an architectural practice. The more important of these affect the office itself and the employment of staff.

Statute 1

COMPLIANCE WITH THE OFFICE SHOPS AND RAILWAY PREMISES ACT 1963
This Act applies to most offices, and affects all 'common parts' e.g. stairs, exists, halls etc. It imposes a duty to register on Form 'OSR1' with the relevant local authority (who, incidentally, will supply the Form).
A number of standards are laid down by the Act including cleanliness, overcrowding, temperature of the office, ventilation, lighting, safety and hygiene. Should an accident occur in the office which incapacitates a person for more than 3 days, the local authority must be notified. This applies to injuries to all persons on the premises, not only staff. Compliance with the Act is not required if the staff are self-employed, immediate relatives, or work less than 21 hours per week. Temporary structures are also exempt provided, amongst other things, that they are not used for longer than 6 months. This means that some site offices would be exempt.

Statute 2

COMPLIANCE WITH THE FIRE PRECAUTIONS ACT 1971
The Act provides that a fire certificate is required for all premises put to designated uses.Among the classes of use which may be designated is use as place of work. The local fire authority will issue the certificate only if it is satisfied that means of escape and other precautions are such as may be reasonably required. When issued, the fire certificate must specify:
* The use of the premises.
* Means of escape.
* Means with which the building is provided (other than fire-fighting equipment) for ensuring that the means of escape is capable of being safely and effectively used at all material times.
* Type number and location of all fire-fighting equipment.
* Type, number and location of all means of giving warning in case of fire.
An appeal against the contents of a certificate or the refusal to issue one may be made to the magistrates court within 21 days.

Statute 3

COMPLIANCE WITH THE HEALTH AND SAFETY AT WORK ETC. ACT 1974
The main purpose of this Act is to place a duty on every employer to ensure the health , safety and general welfare of his employees as far as he reasonably can. This includes keeping a safe work system, giving proper training and (unless fewer than 5 people are employed) preparing and making known to the staff a statement in writing on the firm's safety policies and arrangements. The employees also have a duty to use reasonable care with regard to themselves and their colleagues. An Inspector is empowered to order improvements under this Act, and even to stop the business operating from the offending premises if orders are not complied with. It should be noted that non=compliance amounts to a criminal offence which, therefore, cannot be insured against.

Staff Employment

A STATED TERMS: A contract of employment need not be in writing, but a written contract is preferable as it lessens the risk of misunderstanding. In any event, within 13 weeks of starting a job, an employee must be provided with (or given access to) a statement of the terms of the employment.

B CHECKLIST - TERMS OF EMPLOYMENT
* Names of parties
* Date on which employment commenced
* Wages or salary rate
* Payment intervals
* Hours to be worked
* Holidays permitted, and holiday pay
* Sickness pay
* Pensions
* Notice
* Job title
* Whether there is a contracting-out certificate in respect of Social Security
* Grievance procedure
* If the employment is for a fixed term, the date when the contract expires.

C FURTHER PROVISIONS:
When employing architectural staff, consider whether to add any of the following terms:
* Any restrictions on practice after leaving the employment
* Details of 'perks' e.g. office car
* Requirements of membership of professional bodies e.g. RIBA
* Whether private work is permitted
* The position as to copyright
* Professional indemnity arrangement

D IMPLIED TERMS: Certain obligations are implied in all contracts of employment. The employer owes a duty to the employee:
  (i) To provide work
  (ii) To pay wages
  (iii) To take reasonable care of the employee's safety
  (in) To indemnity the employee against liability in the proper performance of his duties
The employee owes a duty to the employer:
  (i) To act reasonably
  (ii) To work honestly and faithfully, and not to permit personal interest to conflict with his duties
  (iii) To use reasonable skill and care in performing his job, and to indemnify the employer against liability incurred as a result of a breach of this duty

E DISCRIMINATION: It is not permitted to discriminate against an employee, or a prospective employee on the ground of sex or race in Great Britain (although certain limited exceptions apply in relation to sex discrimination). Care should therefore be taken when advertising for staff. It is also not permitted to pay a person a different rate simply because of their sex.

The employer should also consider the position with regard to:
  (i) Rights employees may have to time off work e.g. maternity leave
  (ii) Redundancy legislation
  (iii) Legislation on unfair dismissal

REF PRACTICE MANAGEMENT HANDBOOK. PP. 109-186. RIBA GUIDE TO EMPLOYMENT PRACTICE (1987).

Communication

Letters

- Bear in mind the purpose of the letter, which may be: TO INFORM
  - TO RECORD AN EVENT OR CONVERSATION
  - TO REQUEST INSTRUCTIONS
  - TO PROMOTE GOOD RELATIONS

  This will affect the style of the letter.
- Consider also the impact the letter should have upon the recipient:
  - REASSURANCE
  - CONFIDENCE
  - APPREHENSION
  - URGENCY
  - FURTHER CONSIDERATION

- Identify the recipient and adopt an appropriate style. For example, do not use technical language of an obscure nature to laymen.

- Avoid 'business jargon'. Phrases like 'we beg to acknowledge' have little meaning and may be irritating to the recipient.

- Be concise, relevant and definite. Wherever possible, keep correspondence to one paragraph. However, if the subject matter merits a lengthy communication, use a separate paragraph for each major point raised or answered. Numbering each point (1.1, 1.2 etc.) will aid future reference.

- End each letter on a positive note by summing up the basic intent of the contents (for example asking for a response, informing the recipient of the next action to be taken).

- Use the correct form of address at the foot of the letter. As a general rule, a letter opens 'Dear Sir' merits a 'Yours faithfully', and 'Dear Mr X' merits a 'Yours sincerely'. However, less formal phrases may be adopted when parties are better acquainted (e.g. 'With kind regards').

- Check the contents of the finished product before posting for poor grammar, ambiguous phrases, spelling mistakes and typing errors.

Further Points

- All letters should ideally be signed by those in authority.
- Incoming letters should be date-stamped and referred to appropriate parties for information or a response.
- It is unwise to enter into correspondence with solicitors where legal action has been indicated, but safer to place the matter in the hands of your own solicitors. However, should this not be necessary or possible, all pre-trial correspondence written with a view to settlement should be headed 'WITHOUT PREJUDICE'. This ensures that letters cannot usually be produced in evidence if the matter gets to court.

Economy Tips

- Pre-printed acknowledgement cards are useful in some circumstances, and save the necessity of a letter.

- Window envelopes obviate the need to address a communication twice, and save time.

- Portable dictating machines may also prove useful in saving time, and allow letters or notes to be recorded while still fresh in the mind (for example, on site).

- The development of a file or computer disc for standard letters and/or paragraphs to be used in certain circumstances would save time and provide a consistency of office style.

- Where appropriate, mail should be sent by:
  - FIRST CLASS POST
  - SECOND CLASS POST
  - REGISTERED DELIVERY
  - RECORDED DELIVERY
  - BY HAND

- Stock both short and long headed notepaper, and specify which is required for each letter.

Communications

Consider the relative merits of all means of communication relevant to each task.
Communications may be made : BY LETTER
                               BY TELEPHONE
                               BY TELEGRAM
                               BY TELEX
                               BY FAX
                               BY PERSONAL VISIT

Factors to be taken into consideration when selecting the method of contact include:

- URGENCY
  The telephone is fastest, but telegrams, telex and fax provide written confirmation.
- IMPORTANCE
  Mail may be registered or recorded or, in some cases, delivered by hand.
- ACCURACY
  Written contact is better than verbal to impart accurate information.
- CONFIDENTIALITY
  The telephone is person to person, and no precise record generally exists.
- DISTANCE
  Long distance calls are expenses, but local calls may be cheaper than postage.
- CONVENIENCE
  Letters require a certain effort in preparation and postage, whereas the telephone provides an instant, simple service.
- EFFICIENCY
  A telephone call may not be practical if it has to be followed by a letter anyway.

Due to the ephemeral nature of its delivery, careful note should be made of all communications involving the telephone. Telephone Attendance Memos facilitate this task.

REF
PRACTICE MANAGEMENT HANDBOOK. pp. 101-102, 256-258.
THE ARCHITECT IN PRACTICE. pp. 258-261.

Standard Form of Agreement for the Appointment of an Architect

SFA/92 has been produced principally for the benefit of architects, to assist in agreement of fees, services and responsibilities.

The architect is recommended, but not bound to use SFA/92. It is sensible to include a copy in early correspondence with a prospective client as a basis for negotiation.

The document consists of:
- The Memorandum of Agreement
- The Conditions
- The Schedules

The Memorandum of Agreement

This identifies the parties, states their intentions and defines the nature, scope and cost of the professional services. There is provision for the limiting the architect's liability.
The agreement may be completed by hand or as a deed.

The Conditions

They are in four parts:

PART ONE
This is common to all commissions and sets out:
- Governing law
- Architect's obligations
- Client's obligations
- Assignment and sub-letting
- Payment
- Suspension, resumption and termination
- Copyright vested in the architect
- Dispute resolution

PART TWO
This concerns designs of the building projects during RIBA Work stages A-H and includes:
- Authority for changes
- Statutory approvals
- Third party interests
- Collateral Agreements
- Procurement method
- Copyright - terms of licence

PART THREE
This concerns the administration of the building contract during RIBA Work Stages J-L and includes:
- Visits to the works
- Emergency changes to design
- Contractor's responsibilities
- Contractor's Collateral Agreement
- Architect to issue instructions
- Appointment of site staff

PART FOUR
This concerns the appointment of consultants and specialists where the architect is to be the lead consultant and includes:
- Nomination of consultants
- Consultants' Collateral Agreements
- Authority of lead consultant
- Consultants' responsibilities
- Nomination of specialists
- Specialists' Collateral Agreements
- Co-ordination and integration
- Specialists' responsibilities

The Schedules

SCHEDULE ONE
This sets out the information to be supplied by the client. It is in three parts: ONE relating to all commissions and dealing with such matters as client's requirements, timetable and budget; TWO relating to design in Stages A-H and dealing with ownerships, boundaries, easements, planning consents, surveys and schedules of accommodation; THREE relating to administration in Stages J-L and dealing with matters to be specifically inserted.

SCHEDULE TWO
This sets out the services to be provided by the architect. It is in two parts:

SERVICES TO BE PROVIDED BY THE ARCHITECT
Includes standard services such obtaining the client's brief and, in addition, makes provision for the optional inclusion of a wide range of other services such as interior design, graphic design, life cycle analysis, investigation of building failures and sound insulation advice.

SERVICES SPECIFIC TO BUILDING PROJECTS
Sets out the standard services to be expected from the architect in each of the RIBA Work Stages together with optional services which the architect can provide if requested, such as negotiations with tenants, exceptional negotiations with statutory authorities and preparation of a maintenance programme for the building.

Alternative schedules are available for use where the architect is commissioned in relation to HISTORIC BUILDINGS or COMMUNITY ARCHITECTURE and the content of the schedules reflect the subject.

SCHEDULE THREE
This sets out the method of calculating, charging and paying fees and expenses. It is divided into the following sections:

- Fees
- Time rates
- Expenses
- Disbursements
- Installments
- Site Staff
- Interest due on overdue accounts

There is no longer a recommended scale of fees.

SCHEDULE FOUR
This is used if consultants, specialists and site staff are to be appointed. It provides for the insertion of the names and addresses of the appointees together with the responsibility for payment.

RIBA Work Stages

A	INCEPTION	BRIEFING
B	FEASIBILITY	
C	OUTLINE PROPOSALS	SKETCH PLANS
D	SCHEME DESIGN	

The brief should not be changed after this point

E	DETAIL DESIGN	WORKING DRAWINGS

Changes after this point will result in abortive work.

F	PRODUCTION INFORMATION	
G	BILLS OF QUANTITY	
H	TENDER ACTION	
J	PROJECT PLANNING	SITE OPERATIONS
K	OPERATIONS ON SITE	
L	COMPLETION	
M	FEEDBACK	

Design and Build

A separate set of documents has been published by the RIBA for use when an architect is to be engaged in connection with projects where the contractor is to have responsibility for design and construction. The architect may be working for either the employer or contractor and there is a variety of working arrangements envisaged. The conditions and the schedules are different from those used in the traditional situation and vary depending on whether the client is the employer or the contractor.

REF
RIBA SFA GUIDE 1992
RIBA SFA DESIGN AND BUILD GUIDE 1992

The Codes

Both the RIBA and ARCUK maintain and enforce Codes of Conduct to which their members are compelled to adhere. The codes are similar in content, and both try to provide a general standard of performance and behaviour in all architects to ensure the best interests of the profession and the public.

The principles embodied in each code form 3 sections:

- PRINCIPLE ONE
- PRINCIPLE TWO
- PRINCIPLE THREE

PRINCIPLE ONE

"A member shall faithfully carry out the duties which he undertakes. He shall also have a proper regard for the interests both of those who commission and of those who may be expected to use or enjoy the product of his work."

This includes:

- Agreeing in writing with the client the Conditions of Appointment and fee scales to form the basis of the engagement.
- Ensuring that an architect is in control of all offices.
- Not sub-commissioning work without permission of the employer.
- Acting impartially in the interpretation of the building contract.

PRINCIPLE TWO

"A member shall avoid actions and situations inconsistent with his professional obligations or likely to raise doubts about his integrity."

This includes:

- Declaring to prospective clients any business interests which, if undeclared, might raise doubts about the architect's integrity.
- Not simultaneously practising as an independent architect and engaging in certain types of business (trading in land or buildings property development, auctioneers, estate agents, contracting, sub-contracting or manufacturing goods used in the building industry) unless he declares the full facts of such combined interests to the Professional Conduct committee and that the combination would not prevent compliance with the code.
- Not purporting to carry out independent architectural functions if he or his employer is the contractor.
- Not being connected with disqualified or unsuitable persons.
- Not accepting discounts, commissions or gifts to show favour to anyone, or allowing his name to be used to endorse a product or service.
- Not trying to 'improperly' influence the granting of planning consents or statutory approvals.
- Not continue in an engagement where his interests conflict, without the agreement of the other parties.
- Upholding professional obligations and qualifications in respect of employees, employers and professional associates. This includes giving credit to job architects, allowing participation in continuing education programmes, competitions, spare time practice, professional affairs and (for students) co-operating in practice training schemes. However, employees should not practise or enter competitions without prior consent, in case a conflict of interest arises.
- Complying with Member's rules for Client's Accounts from time-to-time in force.

Codes of Conduct 2

PRINCIPLE THREE

"A member shall rely only on ability and achievement as the basis for his advancement."

A member may:

- Make his availability and experience known by any means provided that the information given is in substance and in presentation factual, relevant, neither misleading nor unfair to others, nor otherwise discreditable to the profession.
- A member may hire a public relations consultant, providing a written declaration by the appointee is given to the RIBA, acknowledging the code.

However, Principle Three also includes:

- Giving no discounts, commissions or gifts to gain employees or work.
- Not quoting a fee without invitation and sufficient information being provided .
- Not revising a fee quotation to take account of another architect's quotation for the same service.
- Not attempting to supplant another architect.
- Discovering whether another architect has been or is still employed on the same scheme, and notifying him of the new appointment. A member who is asked to give an opinion on the work of another architect must observe this rule unless it would be prejudicial to prospective litigation to do so.
- A member who is appointed to give advice must not act as an arbitrator in connection with the same matter.

Misconduct

Failure to abide by the Codes of Conduct may lead to disciplinary proceedings:BY ARCUK
                                    BY THE RIBA

ARCUK
The Discipline Committee of the Council is empowered to hold an enquiry where a complaint is made regarding 'disgraceful conduct' of a member. If the allegation is proved, the architect's name can be removed from the register. However, most complaints fall below the standard of disgraceful conduct and are dealt with by the Professional Purposes Committee.

THE RIBA
Complaints to the RIBA regarding professional conduct are investigated by the Professional Conduct Committee, and if proved, render the member liable to a reprimand, suspension or expulsion from the Institute.

R
E
F
PRACTICE MANAGEMENT HANDBOOK p.31.
THE ARCHITECT IN PRACTICE pp. 23-29

Type

The architect/employer relationship will be affected by the type of employer particular to each commission. The employer could be:

A PRIVATE INDIVIDUAL
A PARTNERSHIP
A CORPORATION OR INSTITUTION
A LOCAL OR CENTRAL GOVERNMENT DEPARTMENT
A SOCIETY

NOTE: Some contracts will involve dealing with both an employer and a 'user', e.g. in a school project, the Education Authority is usually the employer, and the teaching staff are the users. Care should be taken not to confuse the roles.

Effect

The relationship will also be influenced by the character of the project itself. Factors which may be affected include:

- THE ARCHITECT/EMPLOYER AGREEMENT
- TENDERING PROCEDURES
- TYPE OF BUILDING CONTRACT
- STATUTORY APPROVALS REQUIRED
- USE OF NOMINATED SUB-CONTRACTORS
- METHODS OF COMMUNICATION (e.g. who is responsible to whom within the respective organisations).

Contact

The initial contact with the employer may be made:

- BY RECOMMENDATION
- BY REPUTATION (a general excellence or a specialisation)
- BY COMPETITION WORK
- BY PREVIOUS CONTACT
- BY EMPLOYER INTEREST IN ARCHITECT'S PREVIOUS WORK
- BY EMPLOYER INTEREST IN ARCHITECT'S CURRENT WORK
- BY CHANCE
- THROUGH RIBA CLIENT ADVISORY SERVICE

1. The Agreement

The form of agreement between the architect and the employer is very important. Oversights or omissions at this stage could lead to problems later in the project which foresight and attention to detail might have prevented. There are a number of ways in which the relationship can be formalised:

- BY CONDUCT OF THE PARTIES (see page 54)
- BY LETTER (see page 36)
- BY RIBA MEMORANDUM OF AGREEMENT (see page 34)
- BY MEMORANDUM OF AGREEMENT AS A DEED (giving a 12 year liability period)
- BY EMPLOYER'S OWN FORM

2. Changes

If the standard clauses in the Memorandum of Agreement have to be altered, supplemented or omitted, great care should be taken to ensure that the architect's liability is not adversely affected. The provisions of the Unfair Contract Terms Act 1977 should also be noted, as they may render some terms void in certain instances. It is advisable to comply with the conditions set out in the SFA 92 (see p. 30) which should be attached to, and form part of, the final agreement with the employer.

3. Contents

All agreements should include:

- DETAILS OF THE EXTENT AND PURPOSE OF THE PROJECT
- THE GENERAL NATURE OF THE AGREEMENT
- DETAILS OF THE SITE (location and address)
- THE RESPONSIBILITIES AND ROLES OF THE PARTIES
- METHODS OF CALCULATING FEES AND EXPENSES
- TIMES AND AMOUNTS OF PAYMENTS
- DETAILS OF FULL AND PARTIAL SERVICES
- ADDITIONAL SERVICES, IF ANY
- OTHER MATTERS DISCUSSED (consultants, type of contract, etc).

Checklist : Stage A

CHECKLIST : STAGE A

Factors to be considered at preliminary meetings, and possibly mentioned in letters of acceptance and/or forms of agreement may include:

Obtain details of:
- Client and his representatives (names, addresses etc.)
- Project
- Site
- Proposed user

Check:
- The seriousness of the employer and his financial position
- Whether any other architect is involved (if so, inform him of your position)
- The availability of office resources etc.
- Statutory requirements, consents etc.

Discuss:
- Appointment and payment of consultants
- Type of procurement path and of contract to be used
- Methods of tendering.
- Early appointment of contractor, sub-contractors and suppliers
- Methods of insurance and assurance (bonds, warranties etc.)
- Limitation of liability

Provide the client with:
- A copy of SFA 92, applicable scale fees and details of payment stages
- Name of the architect to be in charge of the project and methods of communication

REF

RIBA JOB BOOK. pp. 8-12.
THE ARCHITECT'S GUIDE TO RUNNING A JOB. PP. 8-9.
PRACTICE MANAGEMENT HANDBOOK. PP. 58-64.
THE ARCHITECT IN PRACTICE. pp. 77-111.

Memorandum of Agreement

(Alternative version for execution as a Deed under the law of England and Wales)

Parties

BETWEEN

(1) HUSSEIN CHARGEER

of 1, LETSBY AVENUE, CRINGING, WILTS   ('the Client')

(2) FAIR AND SQUARE

of 4, THE HELLOVET, CRINGING, WILTS   ('the Architect')

Recitals

A   The Client intends to proceed with:

THE CONSTRUCTION OF A PRIVATE DWELLING

_____

_____ ('the Project')

The Project relates to the land and/or buildings at:

1, LETSBY AVENUE, CRINGING, WILTS

_____ ('the Site')

B   The Client wishes to appoint the Architect for the Project and the Architect has agreed to accept such appointment upon and subject to the terms set out in this Agreement.

It is agreed that:

1   The Client hereby appoints the Architect and the Architect hereby accepts appointment for the Project.

2   This Appointment is made and accepted on the Conditions of Appointment and Schedules attached hereto.

3   The Architect shall provide the Services specified in Schedule Two.

4   The Client shall pay the Architect the fees and expenses and disbursements specified in Schedule Three.

5   No action or proceedings for any breach of this Agreement shall be commenced against the Architect after the expiry of __12__ years from completion of the Architect's Services, or, where the Services specific to building projects Stages K–L are provided by the Architect, from the date of practical completion of the Project.

6.1   The Architect's liability for loss or damage shall be limited to such sum as the Architect ought reasonably to pay having regard to his responsibility for the same on the basis that all other consultants, Specialists, and the contractor, shall where appointed, be deemed to have provided to the Client contractual undertakings in respect of their services and shall be deemed to have paid to the Client such contribution as may be appropriate having regard to the extent of their responsibility for such loss or damage.

6.2   The liability of the Architect for any loss or damage arising out of any action or proceedings referred to in clause 5 shall, notwithstanding the provisions of clause 6.1, in any event be limited to a sum not exceeding £ __250,000__.

6.3   For the avoidance of doubt the Architect's liability shall never exceed the lower of the sum calculated in accordance with clause 6.1 above and the sum provided for in clause 6.2.

Dated __15TH JULY_____ __1992__

continued

Memorandum of Agreement (alternative version) *continued*

IN WITNESS whereof this Agreement was executed as a Deed and delivered on the above date.

Executed on behalf of the Architect

B. Fair
_____
T. Square
Partner [3] / ~~Director~~ [2]

_____
Partner [3] / Director [2]

I.N. Terior
Witness Name [1]
6, Attmoy Place
Address
Cringing, Wilts

Executed on behalf of the Client

H. Chargeer
_____
Director / Sec. [2]

_____
Director / Sec. [2]

I.M. Knott
Witness Name [1]
4, "Effercreapin"
Address
Lower Cringing, Wilts.

Footnotes

[1] Under the law of England and Wales, signatures only need witnessing where the document is executed by an *individual*, not a corporate body.

[2] For a corporate body, the signature of two directors, or one director and the company secretary, is required.

[3] For a partnership, all partners must sign except where one has been designated (by Deed) to be their signatory.

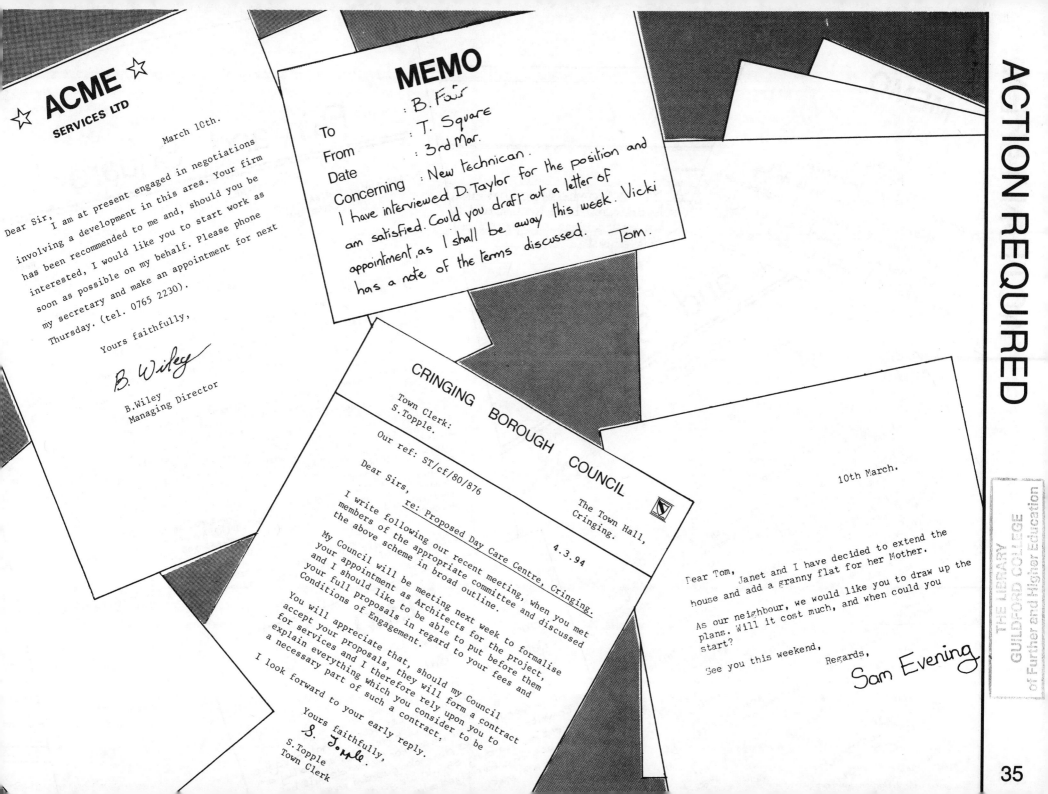

ACME ☆
SERVICES LTD

March 10th.

Dear Sir,

I am at present engaged in negotiations involving a development in this area. Your firm has been recommended to me and, should you be interested, I would like you to start work as soon as possible on my behalf. Please phone my secretary and make an appointment for next Thursday. (tel. 0765 2230).

Yours faithfully,

B. Wiley

B.Wiley
Managing Director

MEMO

To   : B. Fair
From   : T. Square
Date   : 3rd Mar.
Concerning : New technican.

I have interviewed D. Taylor for the position and am satisfied. Could you draft out a letter of appointment, as I shall be away this week. Vicki has a note of the terms discussed.

Tom.

CRINGING BOROUGH COUNCIL

Town Clerk:
S. Topple.

Our ref: ST/cf/80/876

The Town Hall,
Cringing.

4.3.94

Dear Sirs,

re: Proposed Day Care Centre, Cringing:

I write following our recent meeting, when you met members of the appropriate committee and discussed the above scheme in broad outline.

My Council will be meeting next week to formalise your appointment as Architects for the project, and I should like to be able to put before them your full proposals in regard to your fees and Conditions of Engagement.

You will appreciate that, should my Council accept your proposals, they will form a contract for services and I therefore rely upon you to explain everything which you consider to be a necessary part of such a contract;

I look forward to your early reply.

Yours faithfully,
S. Topple.
S.Topple
Town Clerk

10th March.

Dear Tom,

Janet and I have decided to extend the house and add a granny flat for her Mother.

As our neighbour, we would like you to draw up the plans. Will it cost much, and when could you start?

See you this weekend,

Regards,

Sam Evening

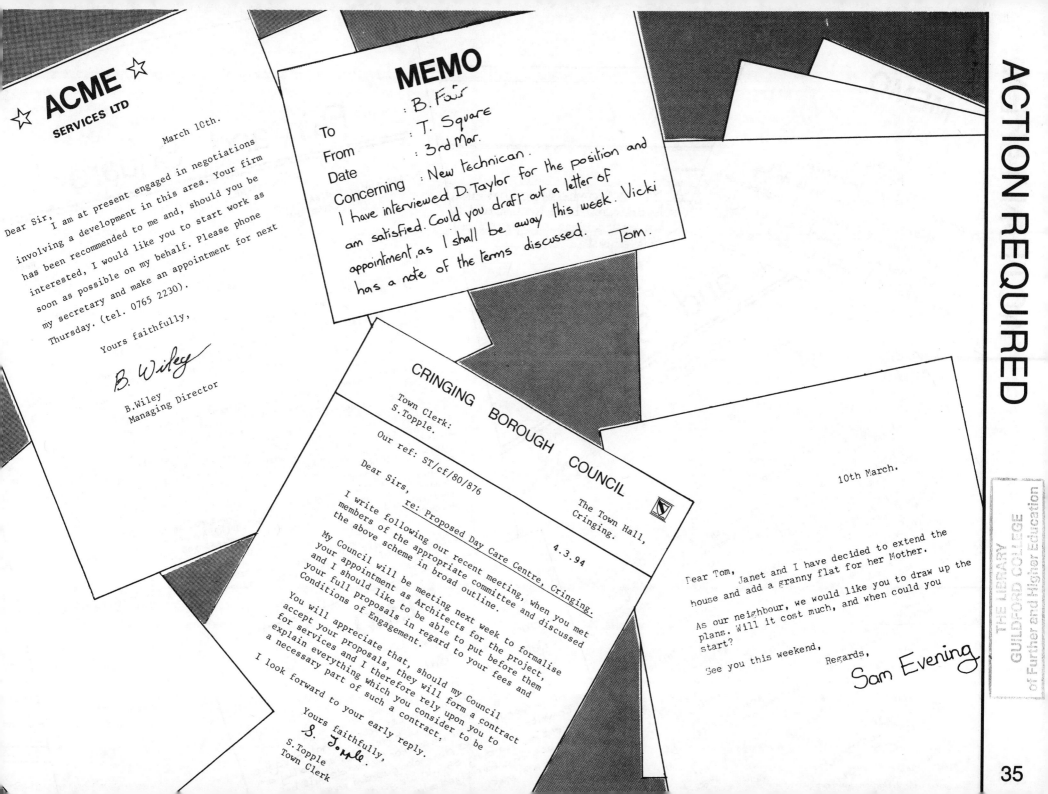

MEMO

: Bill F.

: Tom Sq.

: 12.3.94

Concerning : Work for Friend.

My neighbour Sam wants us to do his extension. I think we'd better not, and besides, we're pretty busy at the moment—can you suggest someone reliable to refer him to? T.S.

A Mr. O. Pforagh-Nuther has asked us to do a new house for him. next to Have used a Memo of Agreement on his request.

Fair and Square

CHARTERED ARCHITECTS

B.FAIR.dip.arch.RIBA.
T.SQUARE.B.Arch.RIBA.AFAS.

BF/vn

4, The Hellov
Cringing,
Wilts.

6.MAR.94

Dear Mr Topple,

re: Proposed Day Care Centre, Cringing.

Thank you for your letter of the 4th March. We are pleased to note that your Council is considering our firm to act as architects in the above project, and write to confirm the terms under which we could accept the commission.

The RIBA Architect's Appointment currently in use (a copy of which we append to this letter) sets out the conditions upon which members of the Institute operate, the services which are offered and a Scale of Charges. We confirm that we are willing to work on the basis of Class 3 scale as indicated in Figure 1 on page 18, which we feel is appropriate to this type of project. If work on a time basis is required, it will be based upon a charge of £x per hour for principal's time and an hourly rate of y pence per £100 of gross annual income for technical staff.

Should your Council decide to employ us, we recommend the use of the Memorandum of Agreement published by the RIBA (two copies of which we enclose) to formalise the appointment, unless you prefer to use a similar document of your own.

Should you require any further information, please do not hesitate to contact us, and we look forward to hearing from you in the near future.

Your sincerely,

---

arch.RIBA.
B.Arch.RIBA.AFAS.

and Square

CHARTERED ARCHITECTS

4, The Hellovet
Cringing,
Wilts.

5.MAR.94

Dear Mr Taylor,

re: Appointment as Architectural Technican.

Further to your recent discussion with my partner, Tom Square, on the 3rd. March, we are pleased to confirm that we have decided to appoint you as technican to this firm. As agreed, we would like you to commence work on May 3rd.

Your salary, details of which appear on the attached sheet, will be paid on the 1st of each calendar month. Working hours are 9.15 am to 5.00 pm Monday to Friday, with an hour for lunch. Initially you will be entitled to 4 weeks paid holiday, exclusive of statutory holidays. Payment in respect of time off for illness, details of our pension scheme, notice, contracting-out certificates and procedures in the event of grievances are all dealt with on the attached sheet, which you are asked to read carefully and retain.

As a condition of your employment, we would require prior notice should you wish to undertake any private commissions.

Trust the foregoing is clear, but if you should be in doubt on matter, please let us know. Tom and I look forward to worki you.

Yours sincerely,
B. Fair for
Fair & Square

Fair and Square

MEMO

To :

From : Tom

Date : Bill

: 12 th March

Concerning : Acme Services Ltd:— What a vague Letter! Are we dealing with Mr Wiley personally or his company? Suggest we ask for further details about his standing, plus make guarded en committing ourselves. Should we go at Let's ask for a fair-sized adv to test him out.

SECTION FOUR

THE DESIGN PHASE

Contents	Page

RIBA
Work Stages
B.C.D.E.F.G

Property Law

Certain legal rights and constraints regarding land may affect a) the choice of site for a particular development, or b) the character of the development if the site is already determined.
The more important of these constrains are examined here.

Land

The major characteristics of land are:
- A. TENURE, the duration of tenant's rights
- B. REGISTRATIONS

A TENURE
A tenant's rights in land are categorised as:
- FREEHOLD
- LEASEHOLD

Freehold property enables the owner to retain full possession of the absolute title of the land for an uncertain duration.

Leasehold property enables the lessee to retain enjoyment of the land, subject to the terms of the lease, for a specified number of years only. (On new leases, this may be as much as 999 years, although much shorter leases, particularly in central London, are common. e.g. 25 years).

Multi-occupancy dwellings must be sold leasehold, where leaseholders pay a specified fee (ground rent) to the freeholder.

B REGISTRATION
The Land registration Act 1925 led to the compulsory registration of land upon transfer in a number of regions. Searching for incumbrances of registered land is therefore less perilous than for unregistered land, where care should be taken to consult all necessary registers. In both cases, however, searches are made in the relevant Office of Local Land Charges.

There are a number of legal characteristics relevant to property that may influence or affect building proposals. The more important of these are:
- BOUNDARIES
- EASEMENTS
- COVENANTS
- TRESPASS

Boundaries

These can be determined:
- By examination of the title deeds.
- By orders of certain authorities.
- By presumption, where no definition can be traced. Examine walls and fences (e.g. fences in built-up areas are presumed to be built on the land of the person who erected them, so that the boundaries are determined by the smooth face of the fence, where the boundary posts are fixed to the other side). Legitimacy may depend upon proving 12 years uninterrupted use.

Care must be taken that all boundaries are settled by the client's solicitor.

Easements

Easements are legal rights enjoyed by one party over the land of another. They can be acquired in 4 ways:
- BY STATUTE, if specifically mentioned.
- EXPRESSLY, that is, by deed.
- IMPLIEDLY, by necessity (e.g. support)
- BY PRESCRIPTION, A person using property in some way may be considered to have certain common law rights if he has enjoyed them for a long period (usually 20 years).

TYPES OF EASEMENT
- RIGHTS OF WAY
  These may be limited as to type of user or frequency of use.
- RIGHTS OF SUPPORTS
  From adjoining property.
- RIGHTS OF LIGHT
  Daylight regulations now fall under planning law and the Rights of Light Act 1959.

Easements are not necessary for:
- * NATURAL RIGHTS, like support of land (but not buildings).
- * PUBLIC RIGHTS, e.g. right of way over a highway.

Covenants

Restrictive covenants concern the prevention of certain actions on specific property, although much of this area is now limited by planning law. A restrictive covenant may be used, for example, by a developer to prevent the growing of hedges or the building of fences by future owners on a housing estate. Care should taken not to transgress any existing restrictive covenants by new work.

Trespass

Unauthorised entry onto the land of another (including the air space to a reasonable height above and the soil beneath) may give the owner cause for an action for trespass. For example, trees overhanging a neighbour's property constitute a technical trespass, and the latter may lop the branches with impunity. Intruding roots below ground may be destroyed and, if they cause damage, may result in a civil action against the tree owner. Eaves projection over adjoining property is also trespass, and an express licence should be sought to obtain a right of 'eavesdrop'.

Trespass may be :
- TEMPORARY, e.g. walking over the property.
- PERMANENT, e.g. building a wall over the boundary line.

If it becomes necessary to enter a neighbour's land for any reason (e.g. to facilitate building operations), a temporary licence should be negotiated with the owner to avoid trespass.
In the case of trespass upon a building site, it remains the contractor's responsibility to ensure the security of the land and the equipment upon it. Damage, even to trespassers may be found to be the fault of the contractor if the site is found to be dangerous and measures of protection considered to be inadequate.
Particular care is necessary where children are concerned, as child trespassers are considered to merit a higher degree of care. See Occupiers Liability Act 1984 Section 1 (3).

Further consideration of the neighbour's rights must be given if the adjoining property is used for some anti-social or potentially dangerous usage:

NUISANCE
Nuisance may be :
- PUBLIC, a criminal offence.
- PRIVATE, a tort involving interference with the enjoyment of land. An example of this would be excessive noise or smell. If a neighbour is seriously inconvenienced, a suit for nuisance to prevent the offending usage or to obtain damages may result.

R
E
F

ARCHITECT'S LEGAL HANDBOOK.
pp. 2,3,8,44-51
LAW MADE SIMPLE. pp. 211-215, 260-287.

Stage B: Feasibility Studies

Stage B of the RIBA plan of work entails the development of a more detailed investigation and appreciation of the employer's requirements and the constraints and conditions that affect them. The preparation of a feasibility study will enable the employer to decide upon changes in the scheme, or consider abandonment before incurring major expense.

Considerations

Factors affecting the project include:
- The type of building (size, character).
- The quality required.
- Special conditions (e.g. future flexibility).
- Time available.
- Finance available (for both the construction of the project and its running costs when operational).

Effects

Careful consideration should be given at this point, as the combination of the previous factors may influence, among other things:
- The method of tendering.
- The type of contract.
- Use of bonus/liquidated damages clauses
- Early appointment of the contractor/ sub-contractors.
- Employment of the quantity surveyor/other consultants.
- Cost studies.
- Studies and work outside the architect's normal services.
- Methods of assurance (insurance, bonds etc.).

Procedure

Physical constraints and the integration of the accommodation requirements will be better understood after the preparation of an adequate schedule of accommodation and a site survey.

Accommodation Brief

The primary accommodation brief should include details of:
- Overall project requirements (function and character of spaces, their juxtaposition, areas and room heights, relationship of international and external spaces.
- Primary elements (walls, roofs, floors etc.)
- Secondary elements (materials, windows, doors, special features etc.)
- Internal and external features.
- Services to be included.
- Installations and lighting (artificial and natural).
- Fixtures.
- Other special requirements e.g. special equipment or furniture.

Building Survey Checklist

Factors to consider when surveying property may include, but are not limited to the following:

WALLS (EXTERNAL)
CHECK: Brickwork (cracks), pointing (crumbling), render (cracks, bulges, flaking), DPC's (bridging) and airbricks (blockages).

WALLS (INTERNAL)
CHECK: Plaster (cracks, bulges, damp patches).

ROOF
check: Tiles, slates (cracks, weathering, slip-page) Hip, ridge and valley tiles. Flashings. roof space and rafters (damp, rot, leaks). Flat roof skirtings, upstands & flashings.

ELECTRIC/GAS
CHECK Fittings, cables, pipes and supply joints.

PLUMBING
CHECK: Hot and cold water systems (pipes, valves, joints, cisterns and fittings).

DRAINAGE
CHECK: Drains, gulleys, manholes, rodding eyes, fittings (cracks, blockages)

RAINWATER GOODS
CHECK: Gutters, downpipes & Outlets (blockages & leaks), Hoppers (blockages)

FITTINGS
CHECK: Cupboards, units etc.

FLOORS AND CEILINGS
CHECK: Woodwork, cills, lintels (leaks & rot)

EXTERNAL WORK
CHECK: Soil, paving etc. (keep below DPC level) Drainage of surface water (away from house) Position of trees & bushes near house

Site Surveys

- Check with the employer and/or the local authority or the employer's legal agents as to title, and any restrictions affecting development e.g. covenants, easements, boundaries, rights of adjoining neighbours etc.
- Check all legal requirements (planning, building control etc.) and establish whether any special permissions are necessary (for example, from the Licensing Justices), or whether any particular restrictions apply e.g. listed buildings or conservation areas (see p,40).
- Check the employer's existing site information, and establish its accuracy.
- Determine the need and extent of a new survey e.g. whether it should be outline or full.
- Decide whether to consult specialists e.g. soils engineer.
- Check access to the site, and procure maps to establish boundaries etc. upon which mark details of boundaries, buildings and special features of adjoining land.
- Where necessary, survey the buildings on site (plans, elevations and sections, position on site and assessment of condition).
- Note special features, general topography and landscape, including tree types and whether they are subject to Tree Preservation Orders (a full site survey may involve taking levels and a detailed site measurement).
- Note orientation and any obvious meteorological factors.
- Record roads (use, traffic flow etc.), paths and routes in and around the site.
- Record services existing on and near to the site, and note their ownership and capacity (the local authority may be able to assist). Invert levels may be useful. Also, note the connections.
- Make a general assessment of all features and structures on the site, and note any general observations.
- NOTE: Sketches and/or a photographic record of the site and surrounding area may prove useful for quick reference back at the office.

Legal Considerations

At the beginning of any project, attention should be paid to the various legal constraints that may affect the scheme. Some will apply to all projects e.g. planning and building control, whereas others will only be relevant to certain types of schemes e.g. the provision of the Fire Precautions Act 1971. Furthermore, some regulations will only apply to projects in particular localities:

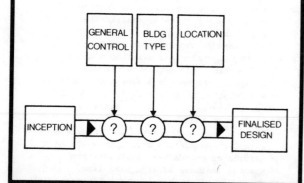

General Constraints

Nearly all building operations require planning permission (see p. 41) and building regulations approval (see p. 45). Most schemes also demand consideration by the architect of services availability, and the position of the employer with regard to the statutory undertakers i.e. gas supplier, water supplier, sewage and highways authorities, electricity supplier etc. In most cases there is a right to connection to main services, but the position should be checked for each particular case. The relevant statutes are:

- For sewers: PUBLIC HEALTH ACT 1936
- For water: WATER ACT 1945
- For gas: GAS ACT 1972
- For electricity: ELECTRICITY ACT 1947

Statutory undertakers have wide powers to lay services on private land without consent, provided that compensation is paid.

British Telecom should be contacted with regard to the installation of telephones.

Types of Project

Particular projects are sometimes affected by specific legal constraints e.g. the construction of a factory must be in accordance with the Factories Act 1961 and comply with the Clean Air Acts 1956 and 1968. Drainage from a factory or other trade premises must conform with the Public Health (Drainage of Trade Premises) Act 1937.

In any premises put to designated uses a fire certificate is required under the Fire Precautions Act 1971 (see p. 28), and nearly all businesses are affected by the Offices, Shops and Railway Premises Act 1963, and the Health and Safety at Work Etc. Act 1974 (see p. 28). Certain types of proposed business premises require licences to enable them to operate e.g. petrol stations, pubs, restaurants, music and dancing halls, cinemas, abattoirs, nursing homes etc. The relevant statutes for these examples are:

- Petrol stations: PETROLEUM CONSOLIDATION ACT 1928

- Pubs and restaurants: LICENSING ACTS 1953 and 1964

- Music and dancing halls: PUBLIC HEALTH ACTS (AMENDMENT ACT) 1890

- Cinemas: CINEMATOGRAPH ACTS 1909 and 1952

- Abattoirs: SLAUGHTERHOUSES ACT 1974

- Nursing homes: NURSING HOMES ACT 1975

NOTE: This list is not exhaustive, and investigation should always be made regarding the construction and licensing requirements in respect of the use proposed.

ODPs and IDCs

OFFICE DEVELOPMENT PERMITS and INDUSTRIAL DEVELOPMENT CERTIFICATES are not currently required, although it should be noted that conditions relating to existing planning permissions are still in force.

Locality

Some restrictions affect all projects within a specified area e.g. proposed projects within conservation areas must satisfy additional considerations in order to obtain planning permission. Some areas are subject to Smoke Control Orders which limit the type of fuel which can be used for domestic heating systems. Restrictions of this nature may be discovered by making the relevant enquiries of the local authority.

In addition, designated Urban Development Areas and Enterprise Zones will have special requirements which must be investigated.

Grants

In certain cases grants may be available to assist in the cost of development.
Types of grant include:
- Improvement grant
- Intermediate grant
- Repairs grant
- Special grant

In addition financial assistance may be available
in respect of:
- Insulation
- Water connection
- Listed buildings
- Compliance with Clean Air legislation
- Water closets
- Certain agricultural development

A comprehensive analysis of the types of grants available can be found in THE ARCHITECT'S LEGAL HANDBOOK (5th Edition).

R E F

THE ARCHITECT IN PRACTICE. pp. 135-145.
THE ARCHITECT'S GUIDE TO RUNNING A JOB. pp. 32-35, 54-55.
ARCHITECT'S LEGAL HANDBOOK. pp. 169-80, 184-211.
PRACTICE MANAGEMENT HANDBOOK. pp. 282-286.

Planning

Planning Law

The enactments of current planning law are consolidated in four Acts:

- The Town and Country Planning Act 1990
- The Planning (Listed Buildings and Conservation Areas) Act 1990
- The Planning (Hazardous Substances) Act 1990
- The Planning (Consequential Provisions) Act 1990

Some procedures have been modified by The Planning and Compensation Act 1991.

One of the major powers vested in each planning authority is the production of development plans for future growth. The development plan is of two types:

- THE UNITARY DEVELOPMENT PLANS in the London Boroughs and Metropolitan Districts.
- THE STRUCTURE PLAN prepared by some County Councils and certain other bodies and the LOCAL PLANS prepared by District Councils falling into three classes: DISTRICT PLANS showing large areas, ACTION AREAS requiring immediate action, and SUBJECT PLANS dealing with specific topics.

Prior to any detailed scheme design, the architect should check the development plan and assess its relevance, if any, to the project in hand.

The architect should also check:

- If the site of the proposed development is within a CONSERVATION AREA.
- If any buildings on the site have been considered to be of special architectural and/or historical interest, in which case, they will be LISTED and GRADED.
- If any trees on the site are subject to TREE PRESERVATION ORDERS.

This information can all be discovered in the

Planning Permission

Before applying for planning permission, further checks regarding the development itself should be made:

- Does the work constitute 'development'? Check the Town and Country Planning Act 1990.
- If it does form development, is it 'permitted development'? Check the Town and Country Planning General Development Orders.

If the preliminary checks indicate that the development will require planning permission, application should be made on the appropriate forms. there are two kinds of planning permission: OUTLINE or FULL.

Outline

This is a useful device to 'test the water', and check the feasibility of a project before too much work has been done. If granted, it shows the authority's approval in principle. Often, only limited information is required, but in some cases (e.g. Conservation Areas), the authority may request additional data.

Full

This gives the successful applicant freedom to undertake the proposals indicated in the submitted documents.

Documents in support of an application for full planning permission include:

- THE COMPLETED FORMS
- THE REQUIRED FEE
- THE DRAWINGS (site plan, layout plan and building plans)
- CERTIFICATE OF OWNERSHIP

The information necessary includes:

- ADDRESS OF THE SITE
- NAME AND ADDRESS OF OWNER
- CERTIFICATE OF NOTICE TO OWNERS WHEN NOT THE APPLICANT e.g. THE ARCHITECT
- TYPE OF DEVELOPMENT
- MEANS OF DRAINAGE (foul & surface water)
- AREA OF DEVELOPMENT
- STORAGE OF HAZARDOUS MATERIALS
- EMPLOYMENT (existing & proposed)
- PARKING SPACES
- PRESENT SITE USE
- HIGHWAY ACCESS
- PERMANENT/TEMPORARY DEVELOPMENT
- DESCRIPTION OF MATERIALS (including colour)
- POSITION OF MAJOR AREAS, AND THEIR RELATIONSHIP TO OTHER BUILDINGS, TREES ETC.
- DETAILS OF THE PROPOSAL (plans, elevations)

According to the type of development and its location, other constraints may have to be taken into consideration (see page 40). The application may be published in the local press, and a decision made by the planning authorities, usually within 2 months.

the application may be:

- GRANTED
- GRANTED SUBJECT TO CONDITIONS, (temporary or permanent)
- REFUSED. Reasons must be given for refusal, and an appeal may be made (see pages 42-43).

If permission is granted (in any form) work must begin on site within 5 years (or other specified period). If the land is sold within that time, planning permission remains valid unless it is personal to the applicant.

Completion Notice

If it is clear that the work will never be finished, a COMPLETION NOTICE may be served. This comes into force after a period of not less than one year from the date of the notice, when all work shown on the approved drawings which is not completed loses planning permission.

Enforcement Notice

If development is started without permission, or without regard to the conditions imposed, the authority may serve an ENFORCEMENT NOTICE, ordering the party in violation to take the necessary steps to ensure compliance with the planning requirements. There is a route of appeal to the Secretary of State.

Stop Notice

An ENFORCEMENT NOTICE may be followed by a STOP NOTICE, halting all work under penalty of a heavy fine. It may also be used to stop changes of use (if it is served within a year, and the change is not to a single dwelling house).

Established Use

In some cases, (where the land was put to certain use before the end of 1964) a CERTIFICATE OF ESTABLISHED USE could be sought, which stated that no enforcement action could be taken, despite the original lack of planning permission. Since 27 July 1992, it has been replaced by a LAWFUL DEVELOPMENT CERTIFICATE.

Revocation

Planning permission may later be revoked or modified, although the order to enable this must be confirmed by the Secretary of State, and persons affected may appeal. Revocation or modification cannot be made where work has started, and in all other cases, compensation may be payable.

REF ARCHITECT'S LEGAL HANDBOOK. pp. 184-211.
ENFORCEMENT NOTICE APPEALS - A GUIDE TO PROCEDURE (D.O.E. & The Welsh Office 1992).

Planning Application 1

Please read the accompanying notes before completing any part of this form.

APPLICATION FOR PERMISSION TO DEVELOP LAND ETC.

Town and Country Planning Act 1990

Four completed copies of this form and 5 copies of all plans accompanying the application must be submitted to the Planning Department of the District Council in which the land which is the subject of this application is situated; the fifth copy may be retained by the applicant for information.

For office use only
Ref.
Date received

PART 1—to be completed by or on behalf of all applicants as far as applicable to the particular development.   Please answer all questions.

1. Applicant (in block capitals)	**Agent** (if any) to whom correspondence should be sent (in block capitals)
Name HUSSEIN CHARGEER ESQ	Name FAIR AND SQUARE
Address 1 LETSBY AVENUE CRINGING, WILTS	Address 4, THE HELLOVET CRINGING, WILTS
Tel. No. (010)01010 Applicant's interest in land OWNER	Tel. No. (010) 10101

2. Particulars of proposal for which permission or approval is sought

(a) Full address or location of the land to which this application relates and site area.

1 LETSBY AVENUE, CRINGING, WILTS

Site Area   0.7   *~~Yards²/Metres²~~*   *~~Acres~~*/Hectares   *Delete where appropriate

(b) Brief particulars of proposed development including the purpose(s) for which the land and/or buildings are to be used

NEW HOUSE IN GROUNDS OF APPLICANT'S PRESENT DWELLING TO BE USED BY SAME

Gross floor space of building if 1000 sq.m. or over   —   sq.m.

(c) State whether applicant owns or controls any adjoining land and if so, give its location   NO

(d) State whether the proposal involves:—

	State Yes or No		Yes or No
* (i) Work connected with a building destroyed or demolished not more than 10 years ago	NO	If the answer is 'yes' will the proposed gross floor space be not more than 10% of original building.	
* (ii) Alteration, extension or improvement	NO		
* (iii) New building(s)	YES		
(*If residential development, state number of dwelling units proposed and type if known, e.g. houses, bungalows, flats)			1 HOUSE
(iv) Change of use	NO		
(v) Construction of a new access to a highway — vehicular	YES	If development does not involve construction of new access or alteration of existing access, please give details of existing access.	
— pedestrian	YES		
(vi) Alteration of an existing access to a highway — vehicular	NO		
— pedestrian	NO		

3. Particulars of Application (see note 3)

(a) State whether this application is for:—

	State Yes or No	
(i) Outline planning permission	NO →	If yes, delete any of the following which are not reserved for subsequent approval
(ii) Full planning permission	YES	1 siting 3 external appearance 2 design 4 means of access
(iii) Approval of reserved matters following the grant of outline permission	NO →	If yes, state the date and number of outline permission Date Number
(iv) Renewal of a temporary permission or permission for retention of building or continuance of use without complying with a condition subject to which planning permission has been granted	NO →	If yes, state the date and number of previous permission and identify the particular condition (see note 3d). Date Number The condition

note: Forms vary considerably between authorities

42

Form App. 1

4. **Particulars of Present and Previous Use of Buildings or Land**

State

(i)   Present use of buildings/land

(ii) If vacant, the last previous use

(i)   PART OF OWNER'S GARDEN

(ii) —

5. **Additional Information**

State Yes or No

(a)   Is the application for Industrial, office, warehousing, storage or shopping purposes? (See note 5)

NO

If yes, complete Part 2 of this form

(b)   Does the proposed development involve the felling of any trees?

State Yes or No

NO

If yes, indicate positions on plan

(c)   (i)   How will surface water be disposed of?

(i) LOCAL AUTHORITY SURFACE WATER MAINS

(ii) How will foul sewage be dealt with?

(ii) Tick as appropriate

☑ Mains

☐ Septic tank (see (c) (iii) below)

☐ Cesspit (see Note 11)

☐ Other

(iii) If septic tank drainage, does the development involve more than one dwelling using a single septic tank (either existing or proposed?)

☐ Yes

☐ No

(d)   What is the proposed water supply for this development?

Tick as appropriate

☑ Public Mains

☐ Private. If private water supply, has the applicant received written permission from the owner to connect to that supply?

☐ Yes

☐ No

(e)   If the application involves a new building or extension please state the materials

(i) Roof   (i) SLATES

(ii) Walls (ii) BRICKS

6. **Plans**

List of drawings and plans submitted with the application   8072/01,02,03,04,05

Note: *The proposed means of enclosure, the materials and colour of the walls and roof, landscaping details etc. should be clearly shown on the submitted plans, unless the application is in outline only*

I/We hereby apply for

*(a) planning permission to carry out the development described in this application and the accompanying plans, and in accordance therewith.

~~OR *(b) planning permission to retain building or works already constructed or carried out, or a use of land already instituted as described on this application and the accompanying plans.~~

~~OR *(c) approval of details of such matters reserved in the outline permission specified hereunder and as described in this application and the accompanying plans.~~

* Delete whichever is not applicable.

Date 19 August 1994

Signed *Fair & Square*

On behalf of HUSSEIN CHARGEER ESQ
(Insert applicants name if signed by an agent)

Planning Appeals

A planning appeal may be made in respect of a number of matters, including enforcement notices (within 28 days of notice), cases where it is doubtful whether permission is needed and established use certificates. However, the most common type is made because permission has not been granted in the terms of the application. Thus appeals may be made against:

- The refusal of permission.
- Conditions imposed upon approval.
- Failure of the planning authorities to make a decision within 8 weeks, or within an agreed extension period.
- Refusal of the planning authorities to approve details reserved at the granting of outline permission.
- Conditions attached to such details.
- Failure of the authorities to make a decision in respect of an application for approval of details within 8 weeks.

Appeal can only be made by the person who made the original application, or an agent acting on his behalf. Notice of appeal (in the appropriate form) must be given to the Secretary of State for the Environment. The time limit to make an appeal varies from 28 days to 6 months from the planning authority's decision depending on the reason for the appeal.

Procedure

Appeal applications should comprise the following documents:

- 2 copies of the appeal form (which states the grounds of the appeal).
- A copy of the original planning application.
- Copies of any certificates relating to ss. 26 and 27 of the 1971 Act, and copies of other relevant certificates or permits (e.g. Office Development Permit).
- Copies of plans, drawings and documents submitted with the original planning application.
- A copy of the authority's decision.
- A copy of the outline permission (if the appeal refers to an application for approval of details).
- Copies of all pertinent correspondence between the parties.

The Appeal

The appeal may be dealt with: WITHOUT INQUIRY
PUBLIC LOCAL INQUIRY
INFORMAL HEARING

WITHOUT AN INQUIRY

The appeal, known as a written representation, is sent to the planning authority for a statement upon which the appellant may comment. The case is then decided by the Secretary of State or, more usually, by a designated inspector. He may, in many cases, visit the site prior to delivering his decision in writing.

WITH A PUBLIC LOCAL INQUIRY

This would be chaired by an Inspector appointed by the Secretary of State, where the appellant and the planning authorities have requested that the matter be dealt with at a local level.

INFORMAL HEARING

This is a simplified procedure having some of the characteristics of 'written representations' and 'public local inquiry'.

Normally, each side in an inquiry pays its own costs, but the Secretary of State may order one party to pay all or part of the other's costs as well as its own.

Listed Buildings

LISTED BUILDING CONSENT - APPEALS AGAINST REFUSAL (The Planning (Listed Buildings and Conservation Areas) Act 1990)

This information is largely applicable where an appeal is made against a refusal by the planning authorities to allow demolition within a conservation area, or alteration or demolition of a listed building.

When considering such an appeal, the Secretary of State will pay special attention to:
- The importance of the building, both on its own and in relation to others (listed buildings only).
- The condition of the building.
- The importance of any alternative use for the site.

and additionally, where the building is in a conservation area:
- The probable effect on the character and appearance of the area.

Definition of 'Development'

For a complete description of what constitutes 'development', see Section 55 of the Town and Country Planning Act 1990. The situation is by no means always simple.

Briefly, 'development' means:
- The carrying out of building, engineering, mining or other operations in, on, over or under land.
- The making of any material change in the use of any buildings or other land.

Not all 'development' requires planning permission.

'Permitted Development'

'Permitted development' (i.e. operations which constitute 'development' but for which express permission need not be sought) is detailed in the Town and Country Planning General Development Orders. Examples are:

- Certain enlargements etc. of dwelling houses. (Erection of garages within their curtilages is 'enlargement' under this Order).
- Erection of gates, walls and fences.
- Building operations for agricultural purposes on agricultural land.
- Erection of most temporary buildings, e.g. site huts, provided they are removed at the expiration of the operations which they serve.
- Certain local authority construction and alterations.
- Certain development by statutory undertakers.

Permitted development rights can be removed by conditions on a planning permission or by a subsequent Direction of the town and Country Planning General Development Orders.

R
E
F

PLANNING APPEALS: A GUIDE. (D.O.E. & the Welsh Office 1992)

Building Control

Building control is a function delegated to the local authorities in England and Wales, where the Building Regulations, created under the Building Act 1984, are implemented by building control officers or approved inspectors. (In Scotland, similar provisions are made by the Building (Scotland) Acts). These are illustrated fully in the GUIDE TO THE BUILDING REGULATIONS 1991. pp. 1-33.

The Building Regulations

The regulations are designed to secure the health, safety, welfare and convenience of persons in or about buildings, furthering the conservation of fuel and power and preventing waste, undue consumption, misuse and the contamination of water. In most cases, where an individual wishes to build or make alterations to a building, he must notify the appropriate authorities of his intention. However, he should first check to see if the proposed development is exempted from the regulations (see Table A). The requirements of the regulations are generally expressed in functional terms and are supported by a series of Approved Documents. However, compliance may be gained by reference to other documents, such as British Standards.

Relaxations/Dispensations

If the regulations apply but seem unnecessarily onerous, a RELAXATION or DISPENSATION may be sought from the local authority (or Secretary of State). The procedure may be found in the Building Act 1984, and appeals can be made to the Secretary of State if the authority refuses an application for a relaxation. TYPE RELAXATIONS may also be granted by the Secretary of State under provisions enacted in the Building Act 1984, which can dispense with regulatory requirements in certain circumstances, and usually with specific conditions attached.

Table A: EXEMPTIONS

1. *Buildings required for the purpose of any educational establishment erected to plans which have been approved by the Secretary of State for Education (except for houses, offices and showrooms).*
2. *Buildings of Statutory Undertakers held and used for th purpose of their undertaking.*
3. *Buildings subject to the Explosives Acts 1875 and 1923.*
4. *Buildings (except dwellings, offices and canteens) on a site with a licence under the Nuclear Installations Act 1965.*
5. *Buildings subject to the Ancient Monuments and Archeological Areas Act 1979.*
6. *Buildings (except dwellings, offices and showrooms) used in connection with any mine or quarry.*
7. *Buildings into which people cannot or do not normally go.*
8. *Detached buildings containing fixed plant or machinery which are visited intermittently.*
9. *Greenhouses (unless used for retailing, packing or exhibiting).*
10. *Buildings used for agriculture sited one and a half times their height from any building containing sleeping accommodation and having no point more than 30 metres from an exit which may be used in the case of fire (unless the main purpose of the building is retailing, packing or exhibiting).*
11. *Buildings intended to remain erected for less than 28 days.*
12. *Mobile homes subject to the Mobile Homes Act 1983.*
13. *Buildings on an estate used in connection with the sale of buildings or building plots.*

Table A: EXEMPTIONS
(continued)

14. *Buildings used by people in connection with the erection, extension, alteration or repair of buildings.*
15. *Detached buildings not exceeding 30 square metres floor area containing no sleeping accommodation and either sited more than one metre from the boundary of its curtilage or a single storey constructed of non-combustible materials.*
16. *Nuclear, chemical or conventional weapon shelters not exceeding 30 square metres and which do not affect the foundations of adjoining buildings.*
17. *Greenhouse, conservatory, porch, covered yard or carport extensions which have a floor area not exceeding 10 square metres.*
18. *Certain temporary exhibition stands.*
19. *Tents or marquees.*
20. *Moveable dwellings under Section 269 of the Public Health Act 1936.*
21. *'Static' mobile accommodation (e.g. caravan).*
22. *Certain engineering structures (e.g. dock, tunnel).*
23. *Tower masts not attached to buildings (not chimneys).*
24. *Plant or machinery.*
25. *Storage racking (unless supporting a floor).*
26. *Amusement or fairground equipment.*
27. *Scaffolding or falsework.*
28. *Street furniture.*
29. *Fences, walls or gates.*
30. *External storage tanks (not septic tanks).*
31. *Prison buildings.*

Building Control 2

Notice of Intention

It is an offence if an application by way of notice is not made, but work may begin before approval is obtained.

Notification Checklist

Notification to the planning authority may be in the format of:

1 FULL PLANS
(in duplicate)
Should include:
- RELEVANT FORM (see page 49)
- THE FEE (unless disabled exemption is claimed)
- DRAWINGS
  - BLOCK PLAN (not less than 1/1250 scale) showing size and position of the building and relationship to adjoining buildings, boundaries and size, use and position of all buildings within the curtilage, width of adjoining streets, lines of drainage, size, depth and gradient of drains and means of access and ventilation, position and level of drain outfall, sewer connection and position.
  - PLANS AND SECTIONS showing precise location of boundaries in relation to proposal, levels of the site of the building and lowest floor level in relation to adjoining streets, number of storeys, position, dimensions and form of foundations, walls, floors, windows, chimneys and roof, details of DPC and moisture barriers, use of all rooms and details of fire protection, means of escape in case of fire, sound and heat insulation, ventilation and access facilities for disabled people. Details of cavity fill insulation and unvented hot water systems.

2 BUILDING NOTICE
Should include:
- RELEVANT FORM (see page 49)
- DRAWINGS
  - BLOCK PLAN (not less than 1/1250 scale showing size and position of the building and relationship to adjoining buildings, boundaries and size, use and position of all buildings within the curtilage, width of adjoining streets. Particulars of the number of storeys, use of the building, means of drainage, provision of exits, building over a public sewer, satisfying local enactments, cavity fill insulation, unvented hot water systems.
- THE BUILDING NOTICE FEE is the combined plan and inspection fees and is payable on demand after inspection by the local authority.

The local authority has no power to approve or reject a Building Notice.

3 INITIAL NOTICE (by approved inspector)
SHOULD INCLUDE:
- RELEVANT FORM (see page 49)
  Initial notice
  Combined initial notice and plans certificate
  Plans certificate
- GROUNDS
  The approved inspector must satisfy the local authority on these grounds:
  - Form of the notice
  - Work is within local authority's area
  - The person who has signed the notice is an approved inspector
  - Location and details of work
  - Approval of his status has been granted by a designated body
  - Insurance cover
  - The fire authority have been consulted where required
  - No professional or financial interest
  - Satisfactory drainage outfall
  - Building over a public sewer
  - complying with local enactments
  - No overlap with earlier Building Notice

NB. The deposit of plans or a building notice is not necessary for the installation of a heat producing gas appliance installed by or under the supervision of the British Gas Corporation.

Time for Decision

The authority should make a decision within 5 weeks unless the parties both agree to extend the period to 2 months from the date of the depositing of the plans. If the authority fails to make a decision during this period, it has breached its duty and must refund the fee, although there is no deemed approval. Rejection of an initial notice on the prescribed grounds must be made within 10 working days of its deposit.

Commencement

If the proposals are compliant, work should normally begin within 3 years of notification by the local authority, although progress rates are not specified, and work can continue indefinitely.

Notices

Local authorities require notice in writing at various stages in the construction process, although they may agree to inspection requests by other means (e.g. telephone call).
NOTICE IS REQUIRED:

- 2 days before commencement
- 1 day before excavation covered
- 1 day before foundation covered
- 1 day before DPC covered
- 1 day before site concrete covered
- 1 day before drainage or sewer covered
- Within 5 days of covering of drain or sewer
- 5 days before occupation if occupied before completion

The local authority must issue a completion certificate:
- If requested at the time of full plans submission.
- If notice has been received that the building will be put to a "designated use".
- If notice has been received in respect of completion or part occupation before completion.

If there is an approved inspector, he must issue a final certificate when the work is complete. The local authority have 10 days in which to reject it, otherwise they are deemed to have accepted it,

BUILDING INSPECTION REQUEST

Please telephone or return this card to advise your council when the work is ready to be inspected for each stage of the works. Note all notices other than the commencement may be given by telephone

Building Regulations Plan Number

Details of work
Location of site:
Builder's name and address:
                                                    Tel:
Signature: Date for inspection:

Stage of work *please tick appropriate box*   **Notice required**

☐ Commencement . . . . 2 days prior to commencement
☐ Excavation for foundations . . . . 1 day prior to inspection
☐ Concrete foundations . . . . 1 day prior to inspection
☐ Material laid on site . . . . 1 day prior to inspection
☐ Damp proof course laid . . . . 1 day prior to inspection
☐ Drain ready for inspection and test . . . . 1 day prior to inspection
☐ Drain backfilled and ready for test . . . . Within 5 days
☐ Occupation of the building (or part) . . . . 5 days prior to occupation
☐ Final completion . . . . Within 5 days

Office use only
Date of receipt: Date of inspection:
Inspected by:

Failure to inform the council may mean you will be required to uncover or remove work and could result in a fine.
'Day' means any period of 24 hours commencing at midnight and excludes any Saturday, Sunday, Bank or Public holiday.

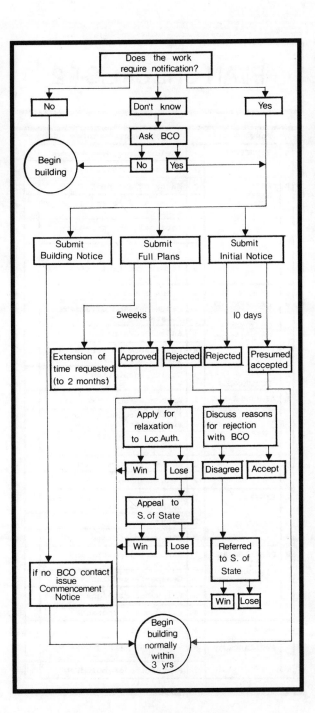

Conditional Approvals

These may be granted subject to the later approval of certain details (which will be listed), for which insufficient information has been submitted to enable them to be determined as complying with the Building Regulations. A time period is not stipulated for the submission of information, but it is normal for such information to be deposited before the relevant work commences on site.

Appeals

REJECTION OF PLANS

The notifying party, if he feels that the local authority is wrong, may refer the matter to the Secretary of State for his determination. A fee is payable for this procedure.

Offences

It is an offence to:
• Commence building without first making a proper written application to the local authority.
• Fail to submit the appropriate notices.
• Build contrary to the Building Regulations and Building Act 1984.
• Fail to submit, in due time, details pertaining to conditional approvals.

The local authority may initiate criminal proceedings, and heavy fines usually result with a continuing liability for each day the contravention remains uncorrected. Notice to alter or remove the offending work may not be given after the expiration of 12 months from the date of completion of the work in question, except by an injunction of the High Court.

R
E   GUIDE TO THE BUILDING REGULATIONS.
F   pp. 9-14.

Building Control 4

PLAN CHECKLIST 1

BUILDING REGULATIONS 1991
Regulations

1.	Title, commencement and application	
2.	Interpretation	
3.	Meaning of building work	
4.	Requirements relating to building work	
5.	Meaning of material change of use	
6.	Requirements relating to material change of use	
7.	Materials and workmanship	
8.	Limitation on requirements	
9.	Exempt buildings and work	
10.	Power to despense with or relax requirements	
11.	Giving of a building notice or deposit of plans	
12.	Particulars and plans where a building notice is given	
13.	Full plans	
14.	Notice of commencement and completion of certain stages of work	
15.	Completion Certificate	
16.	Testing of drains and private sewers	
17.	Sampling of material	
18.	Supervision of building work otherwise than by local authorities	
19.	Revocations	
20.	Transitional provisions	

PLAN CHECKLIST 2

PART			REQUIREMENTS	
A	STRUCTURE	1/2	Loading and ground movement	
		3/4	Disproportionate collapse	
B	FIRE SAFETY	1	Means of excape	
		2	Internal fire spread - linings	
		3	Internal fire spread - structure	
		4	External fire spread	
		5	Access and facilities for the fire service	
C	SITE PREPARATION AND RESISTANCE TO MOISTURE	1	Preparation of site	
		2	Dangerous and offensive substances	
		3	Subsoil drainage	
		4	Resistance to weather and ground moisture	
D	TOXIC SUBSTANCES	1	Cavity insulation	
E	AIRBORNE AND IMPACT SOUND	1	Airborne sound (walls)	
		2	Airborne sound (floors and stairs)	
		3	Impact sound (floors and stairs)	
F	VENTILATION	1	Means of ventilation	
		2	Condensation	
G	HYGIENE	1	Sanitary conveniences and washing facilities	
		2	Bathrooms	
		3	Hot water storage	
H	DRAINAGE AND WASTE DISPOSAL	1	Sanitary pipework and drainage	
		2	Cesspools and tanks	
		3	Rainwater drainage	
		4	Solid waste storage	
J	HEAT PRODUCING APPLIANCES	1	Air supply	
		2	Discharge of products of combustion	
		3	Protection of building	

PLAN CHECKLIST 3

PART			REQUIREMENTS	
K	STAIRS, RAMPS AND GUARDS	1	Stairs and ramps	
		2/3	Pedestrian and vehicle barriers	
L	CONSERVATION OF FUEL AND POWER	1	Conservation of fuel and power	
M	ACCESS AND FACILITIES FOR DISABLED PEOPLE	1	Disabled people	
		2	Access and use	
		3	Sanitary conveniences	
		4	Audience or spectator seating	
N	GLAZING - MATERIALS AND PROTECTION	1		
		2		

ALLIED MATTERS

Building Act 1984

Section	18	Building over a Public Sewer	
Section	21	Satisfactory Foul and Storm Drainage	
Section	24	Exits to Certain Buildings	
Section	25	Provisions of Water Supply	

RELATED MATTERS

Demolition of Buildings	
Dangerous Buildings and Structures	
Fire Certificates for Designated Use	
Means of Excape from Fire in Houses in Multiple Occupation	
Safety at Sports Grounds	
Licensing of Buildings	
House Improvement Grants	
Advance Payments Code for Highways	
Street Naming and Numbering	

Building Notice

BUILDING ACT 1984

BUILDING REGULATIONS

BUILDING NOTICE

This notice is given in relation to the under-mentioned building work, and is submitted in accordance with Regulations 11(1)(a).

Signed ....

Date ....

FOR COUNCIL USE ONLY

NOTE: The building notice procedure cannot be used if the work is related to a building or part of a building used or intended to be used as an office or shop. For this, the FULL PLAN PROCEDURE should be used.

NAME AND ADDRESS OF PERSON ON WHOSE BEHALF THE WORK IS TO BE CARRIED OUT.

(USE CAPITAL LETTERS) POST CODE

IF SIGNED BY AGENT, NAME AND ADDRESS OF AGENT.

TEL

(USE CAPITAL LETTERS) POST CODE

ADDRESS AT WHICH THE WORK IS TO BE CARRIED OUT.

(USE CAPITAL LETTERS)

WHERE THE WORK IS, OR INVOLVES THE INSERTION OF INSULATING MATERIAL IN EXISTING CAVITY WALLS

MATERIAL ....

BBA/BSI CERTIFICATE NO. ....

INSTALLER ....

WHERE THE WORK IS, OR INVOLVES THE INSTALLATION OF AN UNVENTED HOT WATER SYSTEM.

SYSTEM ....

BBA CERTIFICATE NO. ....

INSTALLER ....

DESCRIPTION OF PROPOSED WORK

NUMBER OF STOREYS

ESTIMATED COST WHERE APPLICABLE
£
(SEE SEPARATE FEE SHEET)

FEE		DO **NOT** SEND FEE WITH THIS NOTICE, THE PERSON HAVING THE WORK CARRIED OUT WILL BE INVOICED WHEN WORK COMMENCES.
V.A.T.		
TOTAL		
REFER TO SEPARATE FEE SHEET FOR FEE DUE.		

SEND ONE COPY OF THIS NOTICE, ALONG WITH PLANS AND DETAILS MENTIONED OVERLEAF.

NOTE: A SEPARATE NOTICE OF COMMENCE-MENT MUST BE GIVEN IN WRITING NOT LESS THAN 48 HOURS BEFORE WORK STARTS.

Full Plans Submission

FULL PLANS SUBMISSION

APPLICATION IS MADE FOR APPROVAL UNDER BUILDING REGULATIONS: this application is being made under regulation 11(1)(b)

Signed .... Dated ....

APPLICANT (in block letters) TEL. No. ....

Name ....

Address ....

Post Code ....

AGENT (if any) (in block letters)

Name ....

Address ....

Daytime Tel. No. .... Post Code ....

DESCRIPTION OF PROPOSED BUILDING WORK

LOCATION OF ADDRESS OF PROPOSED BUILDING WORK

What are the existing and proposed uses of the Building or affected part(s)?

FOR COUNCIL USE ONLY

PLAN NUMBER

DATE RECEIVED

Have there been any previous Building Regulations Applications submitted for the project? YES/NO
If YES, Plan No. ....

Has Planning Permission been granted? YES/NO Plan No. ....

PLEASE COMPLETE APPROPRIATE SECTION OVERLEAF REGARDING FEES

SUBMISSION OF PLANS

1. This application is for the Building Regulations only. A separate application must be made if necessary under the TOWN AND COUNTRY PLANNING ACTS or any other legislation.

2. TWO APPLICATION FORMS AND TWO COPIES OF ALL PLANS MUST BE SUBMITTED. (For those applications where calculations are required you are advised to submit an additional copy of the plan, this will expedite the decision.)

3. The plans must include:
   (1) Block plan - not less than 1/1250
   (2) Foundation, floor and roof plans - not less than 1/100
   (3) Elevations - not less than 1/100
   (4) Sections - not less than 1/100
   (5) Details as necessary
   (6) Calculations as necessary (e.g. structural, thermal insulation etc.)

Combined Initial Notice and Plans Certificate

COMBINED INITIAL NOTICE AND PLANS CERTIFICATE

To:

1. This notice relates to the following work:

2. The approved inspector in relation to the work is:

3. The person intending to carry out the work is:

4. With this notice are the following documents, which are those relevant to the work described in this notice
   (a) in the case of a notice signed by an inspector approved by a designated body in accordance with regulation 3(2) of the 1985 regulations, a copy of the notice of his approval
   (b) a declaration signed by the insurer that a named scheme of insurance approved by the Secretary of State applies in relation to the work described in the notice.
   (c) in the case of the erection or extension of a building, a plan to a scale of not less than 1:1250 showing the boundaries and location of the site and a statement—
      (i) as to the approximate location of any proposed connection to be made to a sewer, or
      (ii) if no connection is to be made to a sewer, as to the proposals for the discharge of any proposed drain, including the location of any cesspool, or
      (iii) if no provision is to be made for drainage, of the reasons why none is necessary.
   (d) where it is proposed to erect a building or extension over a sewer or drain shown on the relative map of sewers, a statement as to the location of the building or extension and the precautions to be taken in building over the sewer or drain
   (e) a statement of any local enactment relevant to the work, and of the steps to be taken to comply with it

5. The work [is]/[is not] minor work.

6. I declare that I do not, and will not while this notice is in force, have any financial or professional interest in the work described

7. I am satisfied that plans relating to the work described above have been submitted to me, and that they neither are defective nor show work which, if carried out in accordance with them, would contravene any provision of building regulations.

8. The approved inspector [is]/[is not] obliged, to consult the fire authority by regulation 11 of the 1985 regulations.

9. I have consulted the fire authority in accordance with regulation 11.

10. I undertake to consult the fire authority before giving a final certificate in accordance with section 51 of the Act in respect of any of the work described above.

11. The plans to which this certificate relates bear the following date and reference number:

12. I am aware of the obligations laid upon me by Part II of the Act and by regulation 10 of the 1985 regulations.

Signed Signed

Approved Inspector. Date Person intending to Date
carry out the work.

Final Certificate

FINAL CERTIFICATE

1. This certificate relates to the following work:

2. I am an approved inspector and the work described above was [the whole]/[part] of the work described in an initial notice given by me and dated

3. Subject to what is said in paragraph 4 below, the work described above has been completed and I have performed the functions assigned to me by regulation 10 of the 1985 regulations.

4. The work described above involves the insertion of insulating material into a cavity wall and this [has]/[has not] been carried out

5. The work described above does not include, so far as I am aware, the erection of any building or extension over a sewer shown on the relative map of sewers, except—
   (a) work about which information was given with the initial notice, or
   (b) work about which I notified the local authority on in accordance with my obligation under regulation 10 of the 1985 regulations.

6. Final certificates have now been issued in respect of all the work described in the initial notice referred to in paragraph 2 above.

7. With this certificate is a declaration signed by the insurer that a named scheme of insurance approved by the Secretary of State applies in relation to the work to which the certificate relates.

8. The work [is]/[is not] minor work.

9. I have had no professional or financial interest in the work described above since giving the initial notice described in paragraph 2 above.

10. I have consulted the fire authority in accordance with regulation 11 of the 1985 regulations.

Signed

Date Approved Inspector.

Plans Certificate

PLANS CERTIFICATE

1. This certificate relates to the following work:

2. I am an approved inspector for the purposes of Part II of the Act and the above work is [the whole]/[part] of the work described in an initial notice given by me and dated

3. With this certificate is the declaration, signed by the insurer, that a named scheme of insurance approved by the Secretary of State applies in relation to the work to which the certificate relates.

4. Plans of the work specified above have been submitted to me and I am satisfied that the plans neither are defective nor show that work carried out in accordance with them would contravene any provision of building regulations.

5. The work [is]/[is not] minor work.

6. I declare that I have had no financial or professional interest in the work described since giving the initial notice described in paragraph 2.

7. I have consulted the fire authority in accordance with regulation 11.

8. The plans to which this certificate relates bear the following date and reference number:

Date Signed
Approved Inspector

Initial Notice

The Building (Approved Inspectors etc.) Regulations 1985 ("the 1985 regulations")

INITIAL NOTICE

To:

1. This notice relates to the following work:

2. The approved inspector in relation to the work is:

3. The person intending to carry out the work is:

4. With this notice are the following documents, which are those relevant to the work described in this notice
   (a) in the case of a notice signed by an inspector approved by a designated body in accordance with regulation 3(2) of the 1985 regulations, a copy of the notice of his approval
   (b) a declaration signed by the insurer that a named scheme of insurance approved by the Secretary of State applies in relation to the work described in the notice.
   (c) in the case of the erection or extension of a building, a plan to a scale of not less than 1:1250 showing the boundaries and location of the site and a statement—
      (i) as to the approximate location of any proposed connection to be made to a sewer, or
      (ii) if no connection is to be made to a sewer, as to the proposals for the discharge of any proposed drain, including the location of any cesspool, or
      (iii) if no provision is to be made for drainage, of the reasons why none is necessary
   (d) where it is proposed to erect a building or extension over a sewer or drain shown on the relative map of sewers, a statement as to the location of the building or extension and the precautions to be taken in building over the sewer or drain
   5. The work [is]/[is not] minor work
      (e) a statement of any local enactment relevant to the work, and of the steps to be taken to comply with it
   6. I declare that I do not, and will not while this notice is in force, have any financial or professional interest in the work described.
   7. The approved inspector [will]/[will not] be obliged to consult the fire authority by regulation 11 of the 1985 regulations
   8. I undertake to consult the fire authority before giving a plans certificate in accordance with section 50 of the Act or a final certificate in accordance with section 51 of the Act in respect of any of the work described above
   9. I am aware of the obligations laid upon me by Part II of the Act and by regulation 10 of the 1985 regulations.

Signed Signed

Approved Inspector Date Person intending to Date
carry out the work

RIBA Work Stages C to G

C. Outline Proposals

At this stage it is necessary to approximate the potential cost of the proposed scheme, and to produce an outline cost plan. Although this is normally the province of the quantity surveyor, smaller jobs may be handled by the architect without assistance.

Methods of approximate estimation include:

- COST PER SQUARE METRE BASIS: fairly common and easy to calculate
- COST PER CUBE BASIS: useful because it takes into account roof heights and non standard spaces
- COST PER UNIT RATE: where a price is determined at £x per individual placing or per room etc. This method can be useful when dealing with schools or similar institutions.
- COST PER ITEM; this is more useful where difficult work such as renovations would need to be broken down into measurable elements, and individually priced.

D. Scheme Design

E. Detailed Design and Specification

The specification

- Forms part of the Standard Form 'Private without Quantities'.
- Does not form part of the Standard Form 'Private with Quantities', although a Specification is usually included as part of the Bills of Quantities.
- Forms part of the contract as well as the Bills of Quantities in Standard Form GC/Works/1 and certain other public authority contracts.

The Specific action should be read with the drawings and other schedules. It sets out the precise quality and sometimes the quantities of the materials to be used, and the standard of the workmanship required. Preliminary clauses cover definitions of procedure, responsibilities and general outline of the work. The remaining clauses are usually based on the Common Arrangement of Work Sections for Building works (CAWS).

National Building Specification

The National Building Specification has been produced by the RIBA. It is a directory of clauses covering materials, workmanship and their quality, and these clauses are intended to adapt to each particular project, obviating the need to rewrite the specification every time. It is now available in word processing disk form.

F. Production Information

Consideration of tender action begins at this state (see p. 62).

G. Bills of Quantities

Although often prepared trade by trade, it is now more usual for them to be prepared following the Standard Method of Measurement (SMM 7) arranged in the following categories:

A Preliminaries/General conditions
C Demolition/Alteration/Renovation
D Groundwork
E In situ concrete/Large precast concrete
F Masonry
G Structural/Carcassing metal/Timber
H Cladding/Covering
J Waterproofing
K Linings/Sheathing/Dry partitioning
L Windows/Doors/Stairs
M Surface finishes
N Furniture/Equipment
P Building fabric sundries
Q Paving/Planting/Fencing/Site furniture
R Disposal systems
S Piped supply systems
T Mechanical heating/cooling/refrigeration systems
U Ventilation/Air conditioning systems
V Electrical supply/power/lighting systems
W Communications/Security/control systems
X Transport systems
Y Mechanical and electrical services measurement

Working Drawings Tips

- Estimate number of drawings necessary, to facilitate office programming.
- Draw only as much as is necessary. Time and money are often wasted duplicating data which is adequately covered elsewhere (e.g. in the Specification).
- Can time be saved in the drawing process? A base negative may be used to add "layers" of information onto a duplicated original.
- Decide on a standard method of cross reference throughout the job.
- Organise drawings into:
  - KEY DRAWINGS
  - ASSEMBLY DRAWINGS
  - COMPONENT DRAWINGS
  - SCHEDULES

"Production Drawings: a Code of Procedure for Building Works." BPIC 1987 should be consulted for a fuller guide to working drawings.

- Make sure every sheet contains: (if applicable)

  - PROJECT TITLE
  - SHEET TITLE
  - DRAUGHTSMAN
  - NORTH POINT
  - DATE
  - DRAWING NUMBER
  - REVISION SPACE
  - CHECKED BY
  - SCALES

- Build up a collection of A4 standard details that are likely to be useful on future projects.

REF

RIBA JOB BOOK. pp. 65-94.
THE ARCHITECT IN PRACTICE . pp. 130-184.
PRACTICE MANAGEMENT
HANDBOOK. pp. 282-288

MEMO

To : Tom Square
From : D. Taylor
Date : 18. May
Concerning : Building Regs. re Careful's Job.

MR. CAREFUL phoned & wants b'ldg to start soon. Told him we had planning permission & a builder lined up, but hadn't heard from b'ldg control yet. He said how can we speed them up. I said you'd be in touch.
Dave.

LOCKE, STOCKE and BARRELL.

SOLICITORS

...cke.LLB(Lond).
...cke.MA(Oxon).
...rell.BA(Rangoon).

...BB/bg

1, Fore Hall,
Cringing,
Wilts.

WITHOUT PREJUDICE.

14.5.94

Dear Sirs,

re: New development in Cheapsgate, Cringing.

We have been instructed by Mr Vic Sassious, whose property abuts that of your client, Mr B.Careful.

We are informed that various materials have been dumped on our client's property, and that a large stock of bricks have been left in such a way as to block the safety of his children, who may be in danger of injuring themselves as a result of your client's excavations.

Although our client is considering taking legal action, we are instructed that he is prepared to settle the matter for immediate compensation of £1500.

We look forward to hearing from you.

Yours faithfully,

Locke Stocke & Barrell

Locke, Stocke and Barrell.

Messrs. F...
4, The He...
Cringing,
Wilts.

South Cringing Rural Action Group

25.5.94

...Messrs Fair and Square.

...s,

As President of SCRAG, I am writing to you to inform you of the deep concern expressed by our members about your proposals for a new Day Centre in Cringing. We feel that the uncompromisingly modern approach you have taken is not in keeping with the present surroundings, and will be detrimental to the area as a whole.

Accordingly, we must insist that you reconsider your plans and try and come up with something more in keeping with the existing buildings.

Should you persist in your present endeavours, we will be forced to take the matter to the Secretary of State and our local Member Mr. Gavin Gracefully.

...rs sincerely,

ANN THROP (Miss).

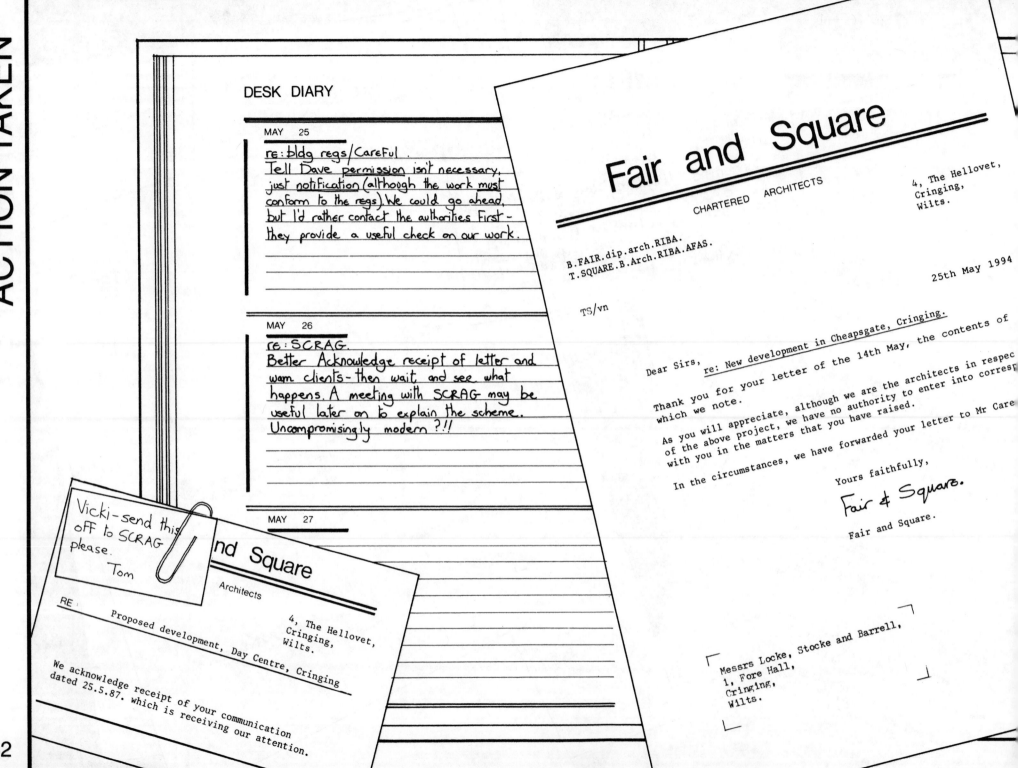

DESK DIARY

MAY 25

re: bldg regs/Careful.
Tell Dave permission isn't necessary,
just notification (although the work must
conform to the regs). We could go ahead,
but I'd rather contact the authorities first -
they provide a useful check on our work.

MAY 26

re: SCRAG.
Better Acknowledge receipt of letter and
warn clients - then wait and see what
happens. A meeting with SCRAG may be
useful later on to explain the scheme.
Uncompromisingly modern ?!!

MAY 27

Vicki - send this off to SCRAG
please.
Tom

Fair and Square

CHARTERED ARCHITECTS

4, The Hellovet,
Cringing,
Wilts.

B.FAIR.dip.arch.RIBA.
T.SQUARE.B.Arch.RIBA.AFAS.

25th May 1994

TS/vn

Dear Sirs,

re: New development in Cheapsgate, Cringing.

Thank you for your letter of the 14th May, the contents of
which we note.

As you will appreciate, although we are the architects in respec
of the above project, we have no authority to enter into corresp
with you in the matters that you have raised.

In the circumstances, we have forwarded your letter to Mr Care

Yours faithfully,

Fair & Square.

Fair and Square.

nd Square

Architects

4, The Hellovet,
Cringing,
Wilts.

RE :
Proposed development, Day Centre, Cringing

We acknowledge receipt of your communication
dated 25.5.87. which is receiving our attention.

Messrs Locke, Stocke and Barrell,
1, Fore Hall,
Cringing,
Wilts.

SECTION FIVE

CONTRACT FORMATION

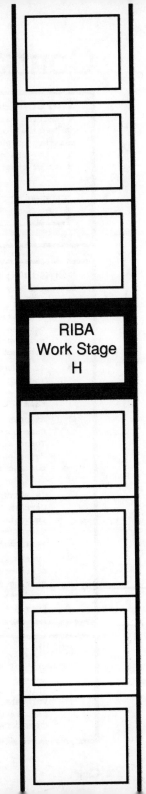

RIBA
Work Stage
H

Contract Law

The contract

A contract has been defined as:

"A legally binding agreement between two or more parties, by which rights are acquired by one or more to acts or forebearances on the part of the other or others".

Sir William Anson

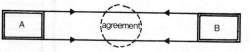

Formation

Contracts may be formed in a number of ways:

a ORALLY
A contractual relationship may be formed between parties in some cases where no written agreement exists, but a verbal contract was made.

b BY CONDUCT
The actions of parties may be such as to prove a contractual relationship between them.

c BY DEED
Some contracts must be formed by deed. These include leases of land for more than 3 years, transfers of titles to land and contracts where there is no valuable consideration.

d IN WRITING
Certain kinds of contracts must be formed in writing if they are to be enforceable. These include hire purchase agreements and assignments of copyright.

e EVIDENCED IN WRITING
Other contracts, for example contracts of guarantee and contracts for the sale of land need to be evidenced in writing if they are to be enforceable.

Validity

Contracts may be:

VALID
VOID, without any legal effect
VOIDABLE, i.e. valid until one of the parties repudiates
UNENFORCEABLE in the courts

Elements

The contractual agreement involves certain rights and obligations for the parties concerned, which may be enforceable in law. However, there are a number of basic elements which are necessary for the creation of a legally binding and enforceable contract:

1 OFFER AND ACCEPTANCE
An offer by one party must be clearly made, and that offer must be unconditionally accepted by the other party. Upon acceptance, the contract comes into effect.

2 INTENTION
This must be shown by both parties, indicating their desire to enter into a legally binding contract.

3 CAPACITY
All parties to the contract must have a legal capacity to do so. For example, minors, persons of unsound mind, corporations etc. may be excluded from certain types of contract.

4 CONSENT
Consent must be proper, and not obtained from either party by fraud or duress.

5 LEGALITY
The contract must be formed within the boundaries of the law. For example, a contract to commit a crime would not be binding.

6 POSSIBILITY
Contracts formed to undertake impossible tasks are unenforceable.

7 CONSIDERATION
Each party must contribute something in consideration of the other's promise. This must be:

- REAL
- NOT NECESSARILY ADEQUATE
- LEGAL
- POSSIBLE
- NOT IN THE PAST
- AND MUST MOVE FROM THE PROMISEE

Privity

Privity is a legal doctrine which recognises that only a party to a contract may sue upon it. There are certain limited exceptions to this general rule, e.g. where an agency relationship exists, the principal is bound by contracts entered into by his agent with third parties. This doctrine is currently under review: "Contracts for the Benefit of Third Parties" HMSO Law Commission Consultation paper 121, 1991.

Discharge

Once a contract has been formed, it can be discharged in a number of ways:

- PERFORMANCE
By realisation of the agreement within the terms of the contract.

- AGREEMENT
Agreement by both parties to cease their contractual relationship.

- OPERATION OF LAW
For example, if a contract is formed for a limited period, and that period expires.

- FRUSTRATION OR SUBSEQUENT IMPOSSIBILITY.
Performance of the contract may be possible at the outset, but be later frustrated by events, (e.g. death of a party, destruction of an element constituting the basis of the contract)

Breach

A breach occurs when either party to the contract does not fulfil his obligations. If the breach 'goes to the root' of the contract, it is treated as discharged, and the injured party may seek one of the following remedies:

1 REFUSAL OF FURTHER PERFORMANCE
He can refuse to continue with his part of the contract.

2 RESCISSION
This is a discretionary remedy, enabling the courts to cancel or annul the contract.

3 AN ACTION FOR SPECIFIC PERFORMANCE
The party in breach is ordered to fulfil his obligations within the contract.

4 AN ACTION FOR AN INJUNCTION
A legal measure taken to prevent further actions by the party in breach.

5 AN ACTION FOR DAMAGES
Damages for beach of contract could be:
GENERAL, that is arising out of the breach.
SPECIAL, for example, loss of earnings.
NOMINAL, if the breach is only technical.
CONTEMPTUOUS
EXEMPLARY, which would be partly punitive.
LIQUIDATED DAMAGES (see page 13).
UNLIQUIDATED DAMAGES (unascertained)

6 AN ACTION FOR A 'QUANTUM MERUIT'.
A claim for a sum for 'as much as he has earned'.

Building Contracts

Types of Contract

A building contract may take any form which is agreeable to the parties involved, but certain proven methods of contracting have been developed which are useful in differing building situations. These include:

- LUMP SUM CONTRACTS
- MEASUREMENT CONTRACTS
- COST REIMBURSEMENT CONTRACTS

Lump Sum

The contractor agrees in advance to undertake a specified amount of work for a fixed price. The inflexible nature of the price may mean that the contractor could fall foul of inflation or unforeseen circumstances, and may be inclined to raise his price as a safeguard. There are two forms of lump sum contract:

1. LUMP SUM WITH PLAN AND SPECIFICATION, which is used for minor building projects and repair work where the requirements are simple and easily definable.
2. LUMP SUM WITH BILLS OF QUANTITIES, which is used in most building work of a traditional nature.

In practice, variation, fluctuation and loss and/or expense clauses relieve the contractor of some of the consequences.

Measurement

A price for the work is determined by measurement and valuation in relation to agreed price formulas and rates. A measurement contract may be based on:

1. APPROXIMATE QUANTITIES, where, on completion of the work, the contractor is paid according to the prices established in an approximate bull of quantities. this method is useful when the employer's requirements are unsure in the earlier stages of the project, as it allows competitive tendering to be used and gives a reasonable idea of what the final cost may be.
2. A SCHEDULE, where the outcome of the work is so vague as to preclude even an approximate set of quantities. Instead, the work is carried out and measured according to an agreed schedule of prices. This method is suitable for minor works, repairs etc.

Cost Reimbursement

The contractor is paid the actual cost of the work, plus an agreed price to cover overheads and afford him a profit. Methods of using this type of contract include:

1. COST PLUS FIXED FEE, a method sometimes employed where a rough estimate of the final cost can be made.

2. COST PLUS PERCENTAGE, where the percentage is calculated on the final cost of the work. This method is suitable for experimental projects and complex renovations, for example. Its main disadvantage is that it provides no incentive to the contractor to work quickly or to keep the costs down.

3. COST PLUS FLUCTUATING FEE, where the fee varies in an inverse ratio to whether the ultimate cost is more or less than an estimate agreed at the outset. This is a useful arrangement, as it encourages economy and speed, but demands work involving cost prediction.

4. TARGET COST. The contractor is paid either all his costs and an additional fee agreed upon earlier, or the value of the completed work based upon a schedule of prices, depending upon which is less. This method requires measurement, valuation and cost accounting.

5. VALUE COST. Here, the contractor receives a variable fee assessed in terms of a percentage of a valuation based on a schedule of prices. Should the final cost be actually lower or higher, the fee fluctuates accordingly. This method tends to be used by larger organisations which have suitable facilities for valuation and general accounting.

Overseas Contracts

British architects are becoming increasingly involved in work overseas. In these circumstances, great care should be taken at the contract formation stage to avoid difficulties which might arise in enforcing the agreement due to:

- Conflict between the laws in the parties' countries.
- The contractual capacity or immunity of the parties.

Before entering into any such contracts, it is advisable to seek specialist legal advice.

Contract Checklist

Some of the more important factors t be taken into consideration when considering which type of contract to suggest to the client include:
- Type of project
- Size and complexity
- Time constraints
- Finance available
- Extent of the definition of the employer's requirements
- Likelihood of changes in these requirements
- Amount of information available at contract formation
- Availability of accurate cost predictions
- Expertise available
- Facilities for measurement, valuation and accounting
- External problems e.g. the constraints on the site, labour shortages etc.
- Quality of work required (e.g. luxury or prestige work).

REF

PRACTICE MANAGEMENT HANDBOOK. pp. 289-302.
ARCHITECT'S LEGAL HANDBOOK. pp. 9-17.
THE ARCHITECT IN PRACTICE. pp. 168-171, 195-196.

Standard Forms

Standard Forms of Contract

Just as any type of contract can be chosen by the parties concerned, so can any form of agreement be used to determine the terms of the agreement. However, in 1964, the Banwell committee found that it would be preferable to develop a standard form of contract for the entire construction industry. Although no such form as yet exists, there are a number of standard forms which attempt to deal with the complexities and contingencies which may arise in the construction process.

Some employers, particularly large bodies like government departments, may insist on using their own form. For example, GC/WKS/1 which is used on government associated contracts places a heavier burden upon the contractor than is usual in private contracts. Furthermore, certain professional bodies have developed their own forms (e.g. the Institution of Civil Engineers and the Association of Consultant Architects).

Generally though, the most commonly used standard forms are published by the RIBA in conjunction with the Joint Contracts Tribunal, and should be used wherever possible. Should the employer wish to deviate from or embellish the conditions in any way, it is advisable to take legal advice on the probable legal effect of the changes before proceeding.

JCT Forms

The major standard forms of contract produced by the JCT are:

THE STANDARD FORM OF BUILDING CONTRACT 1980:
* PRIVATE WITH QUANTITIES
* PRIVATE WITHOUT QUANTITIES
* PRIVATE WITH APPROXIMATE QUANTITIES
* LOCAL AUTHORITY EDITION WITH QUANTITIES
* LOCAL AUTHORITY EDITION WITHOUT QUANTITIES
* LOCAL AUTHORITY EDITION WITH APPROXIMATE QUANTITIES

Supplements to these include:
  FLUCTUATIONS SUPPLEMENT
  SECTIONAL COMPLETION SUPPLEMENT
  CONTRACTOR'S DESIGNED PORTION SUPPLEMENT

Others

Other standard forms include:
* JCT MANAGEMENT CONTRACT
* JCT DESIGN AND BUILD CONTRACT
* JCT AGREEMENT FOR MINOR BUILDING WORKS
* JCT FORM OF PRIME COST CONTRACT
* BUILDING CONTRACT AND SCOTTISH SUPPLEMENT TO THE JCT CONDITIONS OF CONTRACT
* I.C.E. FORM (FOR CIVIL ENGINEERING WORK)
* A.S.I. SHORT FORM OF CONTRACT
* A.C.A. FORM OF BUILDING AGREEMENT
* N.E.C. CONTRACT

'Private with Quantities'

'the Standard Form of Building Contract – private with Quantities' (1980 Edition) is one of the most frequently used, and will be examined in more detail in the following pages.

The form costs of:
* THE ARTICLES OF AGREEMENT (see page 57), indicating names and details of the agreement.
* THE CONDITIONS (see pages 57-60), determining the procedures and conduct of the parties.
* THE APPENDIX, containing dates, amounts, rates etc.

R
E
F
ARCHITECT'S LEGAL HANDBOOK. pp. 57-136.
JCT STANDARD FORM OF BUILDING CONTRACT. 1980 EDITION
PRIVATE WITH QUANTITIES

Dated _____ 19____

Standard Form of Building Contract
Private With Quantities
1980 Edition
Incorporating Amendments 1: 1984, 2: 1986, 4: 1987, 5: 1988, 6: 1988, 7: 1988, 8: 1989 and 9: 1990

Articles of Agreement and Conditions of Building Contract

between _____

_____

_____

and _____

_____

JCT

This Form is issued by the Joint Contracts Tribunal

Constituent bodies:
Royal Institute of British Architects
Building Employers Confederation
Royal Institution of Chartered Surveyors
Association of County Councils
Association of Metropolitan Authorities
Association of District Councils
Confederation of Associations of Specialist Engineering Contractors
Federation of Associations of Specialists and Sub-Contractors
Association of Consulting Engineers
British Property Federation
Scottish Building Contract Committee

Articles of Agreement

RECITALS

Details of the works and of those preparing drawings and Bills of Quantities.

Statement that the contractor has supplied the employer with a priced copy of the Bills of Quantities.

Reference to the drawings by number, and signature by the parties.

Status of the employer in regard to tax deduction scheme to be included in Appendix.

ARTICLE 1

Contractor's obligation to carry out and complete work as specified in the contract documents.

ARTICLE 2

The amount payable to the contractor by the employer, the CONTRACT SUM.

ARTICLE 3

Identification of the architect and provision for renomination in the event of his death or ceasing to act.

ARTICLE 4

Similar provisions in respect of the quantity surveyor.

ARTICLE 5

Settlement of certain disputes by arbitration.

The Conditions   PART 1: GENERAL

1 INTERPRETATIONS, DEFINITIONS etc. of words and phrases within the contract documents.

2 CONTRACTOR'S OBLIGATIONS to carry out the work as detailed in the contract documents, and to the 'reasonable satisfaction' of the architect where his approval of materials and workmanship is required.

The Contract Bills cannot override or modify the Articles, conditions or Appendix. Errors in the Contract Bills do not vitiate the contract, and shall be corrected. The contractor must inform the architect in writing of any discrepancies in the contract documents, the numbered documents or architect's instructions, after which the architect will give further instructions.

3 Additions, deductions or alterations to the CONTRACT SUM to be taken into account in the interim certificate following ascertainment.

4 ARCHITECT'S INSTRUCTIONS must be complied with by the contractor as long as:
1) They are made in writing.
2) They are made within the architect's powers as detailed in the contract.
3) They do not involve a variation of obligations imposed by the employer regarding access, space, hours or order of work, to which the contractor has objected in writing.

The contractor may ask the architect to specify the enabling provision and seek arbitration if unsatisfied.

Noncompliance within 7 days of written notice requiring action enables the employer to have the work done and charged to the contractor (or deducted from the next payment). Unwritten instructions have no effect unless confirmed by the architect or contractor in writing within 7 days. If the contractor complies with an unwritten instruction, the architect may confirm it any time before the issuance of the Final Certificate.

5 The architect (or quantity surveyor) retains the CONTRACT DOCUMENTS, which should be reasonably accessible to the employer or contractor. After contract formation, the contractor is entitled to a specified number of copies of documents (see p. 64), and two copies of any further information that is necessary (none of which must add obligations beyond those in the contract documents). In return, the architect is entitled to 2 copies of the contractor's master programme updated as necessary to take account of extensions of time. The contractor must keep a full set of contract drawings, descriptive schedules and the master programme on site, to be accessible to the architect at all reasonable times. All drawings should be returned at the end of the job, and all contract documents are confidential and must not be used for any purpose other than the contract. All certificates should be issued by the architect to the employer with copies to the contractor.

6 The contractor must comply with all STATUTORY REQUIREMENTS and pay all statutory fees (recoverable from the employer) in connection with the job, and if he finds any divergencies between these requirements and the contract documents or instructions, he must notify the architect in writing, thus absolving himself from liability to the employer. The architect whether he hears of the discrepancy from the contractor or any other source, must then issue instructions within 7 days to resolve the divergence. In emergencies, the contractor may secure immediate compliance with statutory requirements prior to instructions, but must inform the architect immediately. Upon notification, the architect will treat the work as a variation using an Architect's Instruction. Contractual provisions in respect of assignment or subletting do not govern statutory undertakings.

7 The architect determines any required LEVELS and supplies adequate data to enable SETTING OUT of the works by the contractor, who is liable for errors in setting out. However, the architect, with the employer's consent, can let errors remain and can reduce the Contract Sum instead.

8 MATERIALS, GOODS AND WORKMANSHIP must conform to the standards referred to in the Contract Bills or if required, be to the architect's reasonable satisfaction. If no standards are in the Bills, workmanship must be appropriate to the works. The architect may request vouchers from the contractor to prove conformity. Where materials goods and workmanship are to be to the architect's satisfaction, he must express any dissatisfaction within a reasonable time of the execution of the work. If the architect requires opening up the works for inspection or tests to be carried out he may instruct accordingly, but the cost will be added to the Contract Sum (unless the tests reveal noncompliance with the contract). The architect may issue instructions to have work, goods etc. which do not conform to the contract removed from site, allow the work to remain and reduce the Contract Sum, require a variation at no extra cost or extension of time, and (having considered the Code of Practice attached to the Conditions) require opening up the works for inspection or tests to establish similar noncompliance at no extra cost. Work must be carried out in a workmanlike manner and, in default, the architect may issue necessary instructions at no extra cost or extension of time. The architect may issue instructions requiring the exclusion of any site worker (but not 'unreasonably or vexatiously').

The Conditions 2

9 The contractor must indemnify the employer against any liability accruing from infringement of PATENT RIGHTS, and is responsible for the payment of ROYALTIES in connection with the Contract, the sum of which is deemed to be included in the Contract Sum.
However, if the contractor uses or supplies patented goods etc. in compliance with the architect's instructions, he avoids liability for infringement, and any damages or royalty payments are added to the Contract Sum.

10 The contractor must keep a competent PERSON-IN-CHARGE at the Works at all times. Instructions issued to this person by architect or clerk of works are deemed to be issued to the contractor.

11 The architect must have ACCESS 'at all reasonable times' to the site and workshops of the contractor, who must secure a similar right to the shops of the nominated sub-contractors and domestic sub-contractors. The right of access is subject to reasonable restrictions by the contractor and any sub-contractor necessary to protect their proprietary interests.

12 The employer may hire a CLERK OF WORKS as his site inspector, who may give directions to the contractor • only if affecting a matter in which the architect has power to give instructions and then • only if such directions are confirmed in writing within 2 days by the architect, when they become Architect's instructions.

13 VARIATIONS are defined as:
• Alterations or modifications to the design, quality or quantity of the work described in the Contract Drawings (including standards, or kind of materials, or goods, or Bills).
• Addition, alteration, omission or substitution of work, obligations, restrictions imposed by the employer (that is, access to the site, limitations of workspace or working hours and the execution of work in a specific order, but not nominating a sub-contractor to do work set out and priced by the contractor in the Bills for his execution).
• Instructions regarding the expending of provisional sums in the Contract Bills. The architect **may** retrospectively sanction

variations made without permission. All variation valuations are made by the quantity surveyor, who follows the rules set out in this clause. Variations made by the architect in the sub-contract are valued according to provisions in sub-contract NSC/C. A variation (within reasonable limits) will not vitiate the contract.

14 The quality and quantity of the work specified in the CONTRACT SUM is that detailed in the Contract Bills.

15 VALUE ADDED TAX - SUPPLEMENTAL PROVISIONS refers to the VAT agreement (to be found at the back of the Conditions). The Contract Sum is exclusive of VAT.

16 MATERIALS AND GOODS UNFIXED OR OFF-SITE must not be removed (except for use on site) without the architect's written consent, which should not be withheld unreasonably. Once the value of the goods are included in an Interim Certificate, they become the property of the employer (whether on site or not), but the contractor remains responsible for them, and liable in respect of their loss or damage.

17 Provisions for the issuance of certificates of PRACTICAL COMPLETION, DEFECTS LIABILITY & COMPLETION OF MAKING GOOD DEFECTS (see page 88).

18 PARTIAL POSSESSION by the employer of part of the works with the contractor's consent (which must not be unreasonably withheld). The architect must immediately issue a written statement identifying the part and the date it was taken into possession. Possession indicates practical completion of the part & the date of possession governs the Defects Liability Period. The contractor's obligation to insure under 22A ceases for the relevant part and the employer carries the risk from the date of possession. Potential Liquidated Damages are reduced in proportion to the value of the part possessed.

19 The employer and the contractor must not ASSIGN THE CONTRACT without the written consent of the other, but the employer may assign the right to bring proceedings in his name to a transferee or lessee of the works after practical completion. The contractor must not SUB-LET any part of the works without the architect's written permission (which should not be withheld unreasonably). Where the work described in the Bills is to be executed by a domestic sub-contractor, selected by the contractor from a list in the Bills, the list must not contain less than 3 alternatives. Any sub-letting must provide for determination of the sub-contractor's employment should the contractor's employment be determined and for ownership of goods to pass to the employer on payment of the contractor by the employer.

20 The contractor must take responsibility for, and INDEMNIFY the employer against:
• Personal injury or death caused by execution of the works except and in so far as caused by the negligence of the employer or those for whom the employer is responsible.
• Injury to property (except the works) caused by execution of the works in so far as due to the negligence of the contractor or those for whom he is responsible.

21 The contractor must maintain the necessary INSURANCE in respect of injury, death or damage to property and ensure compliance with the Employer's Liability (Compulsory Insurance) Act 1969. He must produce evidence of their existence to the architect for inspection by the employer and, where reasonably and not vexatiously required by the employer, produce the actual policies. In default of the contractor insuring, the employer may insure and then charge the contractor, or deduct the sum from monies due to him.
Where so stated in the Appendix, the contractor, if instructed by the architect, must maintain insurance in the joint names of himself and the employer for: collapse, subsidence, heave, etc. with certain limited exceptions, such as nuclear risk, contractor's negligence, damage due to omissions or errors in design, foreseeable inevitable damage etc.

22 22 A: relates to the erection of a new building where the contractor maintains a joint names policy for all risks insurance.
22 B: provides for the employer to maintain a joint names policy for all risks insurance.
22 C: relates to alterations or extensions. The employer must maintain a joint names policy for all risks insurance in respect of the works and a joint names policy for insurance against specified perils in respect of the existing structures and contents.
The irrelevant clauses, therefore, should struck out.
Where the contractor insures under 22A, the employer must approve the insurers and the premium receipts and policies must be deposited with him. In default of the contractor insuring, the employer may insure and then charge the contractor, or deduct the sum from the monies due to him.
The contractor's obligations under this clause may be discharged if he, aside from his obligations, maintains an insurance policy in joint names against all risks, but the employer can demand documentary evidence of such maintenance or require to see the policy (not unreasonably or vexatiously).
Where the employer is to insure under 22B or 22C, the contractor has the right to inspect the premium receipts and policies and, if the employer defaults, may effect the insurance in joint names. On production of the receipts, the amount is to be added to the Contract Sum. If any loss or damage is occasioned by any insured risk, the contractor must immediately give notice (of the nature, location and extent of the damage) to both the employer and the architect.
Clause 22A states the contractor's obligations for insurance claims.
Under clauses 22B and 22C, restoration of the damaged work etc. is to be treated as a Variation required by an Architect's Instruction. Under clause 22C, the employment of the contractor may be determined by either party (if 'just and equitable') after 28 days, any disputes to then be referred to Arbitration. The contractor need not indemnify the employer, and is not himself responsible, for any injury or damage caused by radiation and other nuclear perils, or to the consequences of pressure from supersonic or sonic aircraft. If so stated in the Appendix, the architect may, (under 22D), instruct the contractor to obtain quotations for insurance against loss of liquidated damages due to extension of time being given by reason of

specified perils. If the employer so wishes, the contractor must take out and maintain such insurance and the amounts of premiums will be added to the Contract Sum. If the contractor defaults, the employer may himself take out the insurance.

23 On the DATE OF POSSESSION, the site must be given to the contractor, but the employer may defer possession for up to 6 weeks if so stated in the Appendix. The contractor must proceed 'regularly and diligently', completing on or before the COMPLETION DATE. Postponement of work is possible only by an Architect's Instruction. If the employer wishes to store goods on the site before Practical Completion, insurers must confirm that such use will not prejudice the insurance. The contractor may then give written consent (not to be unreasonably withheld).
Any additional premium will be added to the Contract Sum.

24 DAMAGES FOR NONCOMPLETION. If the contractor does not finish on time, the architect must issue a certificate to that effect, after which time the contractor will be liable to pay liquidated and ascertained damages at the rate stated in the Appendix if the employer gives a written notice. If the architect fixes a later Completion Date, the employer must repay the damages and the architect must issue a further certificate under this clause.

25 EXTENSIONS OF TIME (see page 82).

26 LOSS AND EXPENSE (to the contractor) CAUSED BY MATTERS MATERIALLY AFFECTING THE REGULAR PROGRESS OF THE WORKS), which are allowed no payment under the contract, are ascertained by the architect or the quantity surveyor on an Instruction by the architect. The claim must be promptly made by the contractor, who should be prepared to show details and proof of the loss, and to supply any other information needed to enable the architect to form an opinion.
Possible claims could be made for:
- Not receiving information (drawings, instructions etc.) specifically requested in writing from the architect in due time.
- Opening up for inspection or testing (unless the work was shown not to be in accordance with the contract).

- Discrepancies or divergencies between the contract drawings and the Bills.
- Work completed (or not completed) by the employer which forms no part of the contract.
- Supply (or non-supply) of materials and/or goods by the employer.
- Architect's Instructions in respect of postponement, variations or expenditure of a provisional sum.
- The employer's failure to give sufficient access (in or out) to the site etc.
- Employer's deferment of possession of the site.
- Approximate quantities not a reasonably accurate forecast.

Certain time extensions have to be notified in writing to the contractor if they affect loss and/or expense ascertainment (26.3). If the contractor receives a claim from a nominated subcontractor for loss or expense, he must pass it on to the architect for ascertainment. the architect will then send a written statement of the revision of the period of completion to the contractor, with a copy for the nominated subcontractor. Any amounts ascertained under this clause are added to the Contract Sum.

27 DETERMINATION BY THE EMPLOYER (SEE PAGE 96).

28 DETERMINATION BY THE CONTRACTOR (see page 96).

28a DETERMINATION BY EMPLOYER OR CONTRACTOR
(see page 96).

29 WORKS BY THE EMPLOYER (or his men) which do not form part of the contract, but information on which is provided in the Contract Bills, must be allowed by the contractor. If there is no such information in the Bills, the contractor's consent is required.

30 CERTIFICATES are issued from time to time (specified in the Appendix) by the architect on work that has been valued by the quantity surveyor. This entitles the contractor to

The Conditions 4

payment from the employer within 14 days from the date of issuance, less any deduction. For example, the retention sum, which is generally calculated 5% unless a different rate is agreed. Any right of deduction exercised by the employer must be notified in writing to the contractor, stating the reasons for the deduction. Rules affecting the treatment of the retention are set out in this clause. The architect cannot be required to issue an Interim Certificate less than one month after the previous one was issued. Off-site materials and goods may be included in the valuation at the discretion of the architect, and on certain conditions (that the goods or materials are finished, insured, clearly marked, and that proof can be shown of their ownership and destination). Not later than 6 months after Practical Completion, the contractor must submit all necessary documents for final adjustment of the Contract Sum. Within 3 months thereafter, the quantity surveyor must complete any ascertainment of loss and/or expense, prepare final adjustment of the Contract Sum, and send details to the contractor. The items to be included in the adjustment are set out in this clause (30.6).

As soon as practical (but not less than 28 days prior to the issue of the Final Certificate) the architect must issue an Interim Certificate showing the final adjustment of nominated sub-contractor sums. The Final Certificate is issued before 2 months has expired from either the end of the Defects Liability period, issue of Making Good of Defects Certificate or sending of adjustment statement to the contractor. The Final Certificate must be honoured within 28 days and is conclusive that:

- Work is to the architect's reasonable satisfaction.
- All the financial provisions of the contract have been observed.
- All due extensions of time have been given.
- Reimbursement under clause 26.1 is in final settlement of all claims arising out of clause 26.2 for breach of contract or in tort.

3
1 FINANCE (No.2) ACT 1975 - STATUTORY TAX DEDUCTION SCHEME. This only applies to employees who are 'contractors' for purposes of the Act, ensuring that the contractor tell employers whether or not statutory deductions are to be made, and giving proof of reasons for non-deductions if necessary. If deductions are to be made, the contractor must inform the employer and send the architect a copy.

3
4 ANTIQUITIES, upon discovery, become the property of the employer, and the contractor must try to protect and preserve any findings, informing the architect (or clerk of works), who will issue instructions on the matter. If these result in direct loss or expense to the contractor, the architect may ascertain the amount and add it to the Contract Sum. (An extension of time may also be allowed).

PART TWO: NOMINATED SUB-CONTRACTORS AND NOMINATED SUPPLIERS (see page 66).

PART THREE: FLUCTUATIONS

PART FOUR: SETTLEMENT OF DISPUTES - ARBITRATION (see page 97).

APPENDIX, containing dates, figures, rates, rules, time allowances etc.

SUPPLEMENTAL PROVISIONS (the VAT agreement).

R
E
F   JCT Standard Form of Building Contract 1980 Edition. Private with Quantities.

Appendix

	Clause etc.	
Statutory tax deduction scheme – Finance (No. 2) Act 1975	Fourth recital and 31	Employer at Base Date *is a 'contractor'/is not a 'contractor' for the purposes of the Act and the Regulations *(Delete as applicable)
Base Date	1·3	29 Jan 1993
Date for completion	1·3	17 Dec 1993
VAT Agreement	15·2	Clause 1A of the VAT Agreement ~~applies~~/does not apply [k·1] *(Delete as applicable)
Defects Liability Period (if none other stated is 6 months from the day named in the Certificate of Practical Completion of the Works)	17·2	6 MONTHS
Assignment by Employer of benefits after Practical Completion	19·1·2	Clause 19·1·2 *applies/~~does not apply~~ *(Delete as applicable)
Insurance cover for any one occurrence or series of occurrences arising out of one event	21·1·1	£ X00,000
Insurance – liability of Employer	21·2·1	Insurance *may be required/~~is not required~~ Amount of indemnity for any one occurrence or series of occurrences arising out of one event £ X00,000 [y·1] *(Delete as applicable)
Insurance of the Works – alternative clauses	22·1	*Clause 22A/~~Clause 22B~~/~~Clause 22C~~ applies (See Footnote [m] to Clause 22) *(Delete as applicable)
Percentage to cover professional fees	*22A ~~22B~~ ~~22C·2~~ *(Delete as applicable)	10%

	Clause etc.	
Annual renewal date of insurance as supplied by Contractor	22A·3·1	NOT APPLICABLE
Insurance for Employer's loss of liquidated damages – clause 25·4·3	22D	Insurance ~~may be required/~~is not required *(Delete as applicable)
	22D·2	Period of time — — —
Date of Possession	23·1·1	1 FEBRUARY 1993
Deferment of the Date of Possession	23·1·2 25·4·13 26·1	Clause 23·1·2 *applies/~~does not apply~~ Period of deferment if it is to be less than 6 weeks is 4 WEEKS *(Delete as applicable)
Liquidated and ascertained damages	24·2	at the rate of £150.00 per WEEK
Period of delay: [z·1]	28·1·3	ONE MONTH
Period of delay: [z·2]	28A·1·1 28A·1·3	ONE MONTH
Period of delay: [z·3]	28A·1·2	THREE MONTHS
Period of Interim Certificates (if none stated is one month)	30·1·3	ONE MONTH
Retention Percentage (if less than 5 per cent) [aa]	30·4·1·1	5%
Work reserved for Nominated Sub-Contractors for which the Contractor desires to tender	35·2	NONE
Fluctuations: (if alternative required is not shown clause 38 shall apply)	37	clause 38 [cc] ~~clause 39~~ ~~clause 40~~
Percentage addition	38·7 or 39·8	X%
Formula Rules	40·1·1·1	NOT APPLICABLE
	rule 3	Base Month _____ 19___
	rules 10 and 30 (i)	Part I/Part II [dd] of Section 2 of the Formula Rules is to apply

It is essential that periods be inserted since otherwise no period of delay would be prescribed.

	Clause etc.	
Settlement of disputes – Arbitration – appointor (if no appointor is selected the appointor shall be the President or a Vice-President, Royal Institute of British Architects)	41·1	President or a Vice-President: *Royal Institute of British Architects ~~Royal Institution of Chartered Surveyors~~ ~~Chartered Institute of Arbitrators~~ *(Delete as applicable)
Settlement of disputes – Arbitration	41·2	Clauses 41·2·1 and 41·2·2 apply (See clause 41·2·3)

Footnotes

[k·1] Clause 1A can only apply where the Contractor is satisfied at the date the Contract is entered into that his output tax on all supplies to the Employer under the Contract will be at either a positive or a zero rate of tax.

On and from 1 April 1989 the supply in respect of a building designed for a 'relevant residential purpose' or for a 'relevant charitable purpose' (as defined in the legislation which gives statutory effect to the VAT changes operative from 1 April 1989) is only zero rated if the person to whom the supply is made has given to the Contractor a certificate in statutory form: see the VAT leaflet 708 revised 1989. Where a contract supply is zero rated by certificate only the person holding the certificate (usually the Contractor) may zero rate his supply.

This footnote repeats footnote [k·1] for clause 15·2

[y·1] If the indemnity is to be for an aggregate amount and not for any one occurrence or series of occurrences the entry should make this clear.

Footnotes

[z] It is suggested that the periods should be:
z·1 one month;
z·2 one month;
z·3 three months.

[aa] The percentage will be 5 per cent unless a lower rate is specified here.

[bb] Not used.

[cc] Delete alternatives not used.

[dd] Strike out according to which method of formula adjustment (Part I – Work Category Method or Part II – Work Group Method) has been stated in the documents issued to tenderers.

Tender Action 1

Tendering

At certain points in the design process, it is necessary to consider the appointment of a suitable contractor to undertake the building work. The choice may be made:

- BY NEGOTIATION
- BY COMPETITION

Negotiation

This follows the procedure laid out in 'The Code of Procedure for Two Stage Selective Tendering' (1983)

NEGOTIATED CONTRACTS

In certain circumstances, it may be advantageous to bring the contractor into the project on a non-competitive basis:

- Where time for construction is limited.
- Where specialised building techniques are involved which can only be undertaken by certain contractors.
- Where the contractor's expertise in a particular situation would be valuable.
- Where the contractor has an established working relationship with the employer.
- Where the project involves additional work to a site where there is an ongoing contract with a contractor.

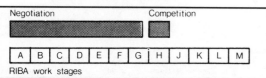

Negotiation   Competition

| A | B | C | D | E | F | G | H | J | K | L | M |

RIBA work stages

A shortlist of suitable contractors can be drawn up, or a specific contractor approached. It is necessary to establish a basis for a negotiated contract, which could be:

- A SCHEDULE OF PRICES
- AN APPROXIMATE BILL
- A PRICED BILL OF A RECENTLY COMPLETED PROJECT UNDERTAKEN BY THE CONTRACTOR

When terms have been negotiated, the employer may send the contractor a LETTER OF INTENT, but only after having specialist advice. It is better, if possible, to enter into a formal contract at this stage, because letters of intent can have unforeseen consequences.

Competition

SELECTIVE OR COMPETITIVE TENDERING

This allows the procedure laid out in "The Code of Procedure for Single Stage Selective Tendering" (revised 1989) or, if appropriate, "The Code of Procedure for Selective Tendering for Design and Rebuild" (1985)

1. The Shortlist

Selection of a shortlist from:

- CLIENT'S APPROVED LIST
- PERSONAL EXPERIENCE
- RESEARCH OR RECOMMENDATION

Based upon the firm's:

- EXPERIENCE AND REPUTATION
- FINANCIAL STATUS
- SUITABILITY FOR THE PROJECT
- CURRENT AVAILABILITY

Checked by:

- QUESTIONNAIRE
- REFERENCES
- PROOF OF FINANCIAL STATUS
- INSPECTION OF PREVIOUS OR PRESENT WORK
- VISIT TO WORKSHOPS

The number on the shortlist should be no more than 6.

SIZE OF CONTRACT	MAXIMUM NUMBER OF TENDERERS
Up to £50,000	5
£50,000-£250,000	6
£250,000-£1 million	8
£1 million +	6

although two reserve names should be appended to the list.

2. Preliminary Enquiry

Issuance of the PRELIMINARY ENQUIRY FOR INVITATION TO TENDER.

This should give details of:

- The project and its location
- The parties involved (including nominated sub-contractors)
- Approximate cost range
- Type of contract to be used (and whether as a deed or under hand)
- Time stipulations (commencement, completion etc.)
- Date of tender document dispatch
- Tender period
- Liquidated damages
- Bond requirements
- Correction of priced bills
- Further conditions, if any

It is usual to allow 4 to 6 weeks before issuing tender documents. If during this time a firm agrees to participate in tendering procedures, the agreement should be honoured or, if necessary, revoked not later than 2 days after the issuance of the tender documents.

3. Invitation to Tender

When the final time for acceptance has passed, a final shortlist of contractors is drawn up, and the unsuccessful parties notified. The contractors placed on the shortlist are then issued:

- A Formal Invitation to Tender
- A Form of Tender (2 copies)
- The necessary drawings
- Bill(s) of Quantities (2 copies) or, where none, a specification
- Addressed envelopes for the returned tenders
- Addressed envelope for the return of the drawings etc.
- Instructions regarding drawing inspection and site inspection
- A covering letter

The employer and the quantity surveyor should also be sent copies of the letter and specification, if used.

Formal Invitation to Tender

Dear Sirs,
      re: New development at ....

Following your acceptance of the invitation to tender for the above, we now have pleasure in enclosing the following:

A. Two copies of the bills of quantities.
B. Two copies of the general arrangement drawings indicating the general character, shape and disposition of the works.
C. Two copies of the form of tender.
D. Addressed envelopes for the return of the tender and instructions relating thereto.

Will you please also note:
1. Drawings and details may be inspected at ....
2. The site may be inspected by arrangement with ourselves.
3. Tendering procedure will be in accordance with the principles of the 'Code of Procedure for Single Stage Selective Tendering 1989'.
4. Examination and adjustment of priced bills (Section 6 of the Code), Alternative 1/2 (delete as appropriate) will apply.

The completed form of tender is to be sealed in the endorsed envelope provided and delivered or sent by post to reach this office not later than .....hours on ..... the ..... day of ..... 19...

Will you please acknowledge receipt of this letter and enclosures and confirm that you are able to submit a tender in accordance with these instructions?
      Yours faithfully,

      ....
      Architect/Quantity surveyor

Form of Tender

This form of tender is used only when a formal contract is entered into.

TENDER FOR _____

TO _____

Sir,
    We having read the conditions of contract and bills of quantities delivered to us and having examined the drawings referred to therein do hereby offer to execute and complete in accordance with the conditions of contract the whole of the works described for the sum of £........ and within ...... weeks from the date of possession (note: this last insert will be filled in before the Form is sent).

We agree that should obvious errors in pricing or errors in arithmetic be discovered before acceptance of this offer in the priced bills of quantities submitted by us these errors will be dealt with in accordance with Alternative 1/2 (delete as appropriate) contained in Section 6 of the 'Code of Procedure for Single Stage Selective Tendering 1989'.

This tender remains open for consideration for ..... days (note: not normally more than 28 days) from the date fixed for the submission or lodgement of tenders.

Dated this ..... day of .... 19....

Name ....

Address ....

Signature ....

4. Time Allowed

The time allowed for tendering depends upon the time and complexity of the project, but should not be less than 4 weeks. If any problems or discrepancies are found in the tender documents, the architect should be notified not less than 10 days before the opening, so that an extension may be granted if the documents need to be amended.

5. The Opening

Tenders are opened on the specified date, and any later entries should be promptly returned unopened. Although it is usual for the lowest bid to be accepted, the employer is not bound to follow this. All unsuccessful parties should be promptly notified except for the next two lowest bids (who are informed of their position) and the lowest (generally) who should be asked to submit priced bills of quantities within 4 working days for the quantity surveyor to check for errors.

Errors

Errors may be dealt with in 2 ways:
- **ALTERNATIVE 1**, where the tenderer may withdraw his offer, or confirm and agree to an endorsement of the bills.
- **ALTERNATIVE 2**, where the tenderer is allowed to correct genuine errors. However, if the correction causes the base bid to rise above the next lowest bid, the latter will then be examined. If he opts not to amend his offer an endorsement may also be used in this alternative.
In the event that the lowest tenderer exceeds the budget available, negotiations may be entered into by the parties with a view to making reductions.

Once the contract is let, all the tenderers should be sent a list of the comparative tender prices. Care should be taken to ensure all drawings and bills have been returned.
Prior to building commencement, there is a recommended period of detailed project planning and organisation. However, although very important, this period should not be unnecessarily long, as extra costs could be incurred as a result of the delay.

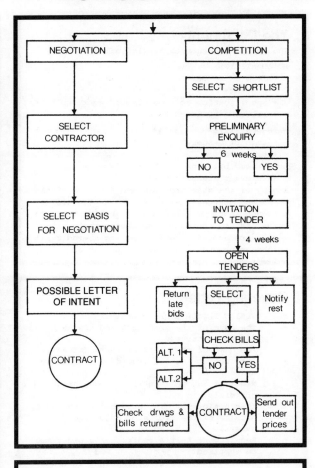

Serial Tenders

These are used for successive phases of the same project or for work involving standardised designs, where the contractor agrees to enter into a series of lump sum contracts.

R E F
RIBA JOB GOOD. pp. 95-97.
PRACTICE MANAGEMENT
HANDBOOK. pp. 242-246.
THE ARCHITECT'S GUIDE TO RUNNING
A JOB. pp. 84-85, 94-99.
THE ARCHITECT IN PRACTICE. pp. 184-194.

Contract Formation 1

The Documents

The contract documents consist of:

NO QUANTITIES

- form of tender
- drawings
- specification or schedules of work (if any)
- relevant standard form

WITH QUANTITIES

- form of tender
- drawings
- priced bills of quantities
- relevant standard form

A copy of the standard form and 2 copies of the bills and drawings, with copies of all relevant consents, notices, licences and building notice cards and top copies of sub-contractor's estimates, are sent (preferably by registered mail) to the contractor with a covering letter.

Covering Letter

The COVERING LETTER might contain:

- The name of the architect and how he can be contacted.
- The name of the clerk of works (if any).
- Instructions on the procedure if queries arise.
- Names of any relevant local government officials.
- Instructions on site possession (including details of the rights of adjoining owners).
- Requirement that a contractor's programme be supplied.
- Request for details of relevant insurance policies and premium receipts.

Other matters which require attention at contract formation include:

- Details of site meetings, including the date of the first site meeting (see p 74).
- Provisions for contractor/sub-contractor meetings.
- Details of site huts etc.
- Pre-orders for materials.
- Procedures for exchange of information.
- Signboards, security, etc.

NOTE: if the site is formally handed over to the contractor at commencement of the contract, immediate problems or queries can be dealt with at the same time.

The Programme

The master programme is referred to in Clause 5 of the contract (see page 57). The Contract Bills or Specification should state the type of programme required:

Gantt (or Bar) Chart

The individual bars represent specific work areas, while their lengths indicate periods of time involved. This is the simplest type of programme, easily understood and favoured by many site personnel. the bar chart is suitable for simple jobs, is easy to monitor in terms of progress, but does not reflect the reasons for delays very easily.

Network Analysis

Activities are represented by arrows converging to, and diverging from, EVENT points. Times are indicated by figures, and the programme is suitable for all types of projects. More complex work may require a computer to update and monitor progress. The CRITICAL PATH and float can be readily determined, and actual and potential delays identified.

Precedence Diagram

This is similar in principle to NETWORK ANALYSIS. Activities are shown in boxes together with duration times and float, so that the CRITICAL PATH can be determined. It is relatively easy to understand, and is capable of containing a considerable amount of useful information.

Line of Balance

This is only suitable for projects containing a number of similar units (e.g. housing). The chart has three points of reference:

- Units
- Specific work areas
- Time

It is useful for providing an overview of a scheme, but is not easy to update or to record progress.

Use of Computers

It is now usual for even relatively small projects to be programmed using sophisticated network or precedent techniques.

There are several excellent software packages which simplify the construction of such a network and permit the information to be plotted in optional program formats.

Once the program is in the computer, the task of updating and of predicting the results of delays or accelerations is simplified. These techniques are widely used by or on behalf of contractors when submitting claims and by architects in estimating extensions of time or assessing the validity of the contractor's assertions.

The computer will still produce a simple bar chart for use on site alongside highly detailed delineations of critical paths and earliest and latest start and finish dates.

Contract Formation 2

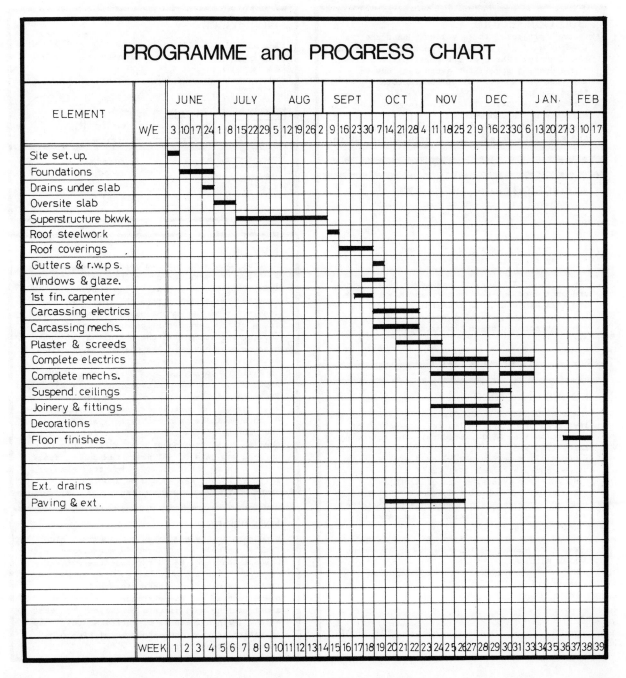

PROGRAMME and PROGRESS CHART

ELEMENT	W/E	JUNE				JULY				AUG				SEPT				OCT				NOV				DEC				JAN.				FEB	
		3	10	17	24	1	8	15	22	29	5	12	19	26	2	9	16	23	30	7	14	21	28	4	11	18	25	2	9	16	23	30	6	13	20	27	3	10	17
Site set. up.		▬																																					
Foundations			▬																																			
Drains under slab					▬																																	
Oversite slab							▬																															
Superstructure bkwk.									▬▬▬▬▬																												
Roof steelwork															▬																							
Roof coverings																	▬▬																					
Gutters & r.w.p s.																		▬																				
Windows & glaze.																				▬																		
1st fin. carpenter																				▬																		
Carcassing electrics																						▬▬																
Carcassing mechs.																							▬▬															
Plaster & screeds																									▬▬													
Complete electrics																											▬▬▬		▬▬▬								
Complete mechs.																										▬▬▬		▬▬▬									
Suspend. ceilings																														▬▬								
Joinery & fittings																													▬▬▬									
Decorations																															▬▬▬▬						
Floor finishes																																			▬		
Ext. drains					▬▬▬																																	
Paving & ext.																			▬▬▬▬																		

WEEK	1	2	3	4	5	6	7	8	9	10	11	12	13	14	15	16	17	18	19	20	21	22	23	24	25	26	27	28	29	30	31	32	33	34	35	36	37	38	39

Sub-Contractors/Suppliers

Sub-Contractors

On many projects, it is unlikely that the contractor will carry out all the work required by the contract. Parts of the work, particularly those needing specialist attention, may be assigned or sub-let to sub-contractors. These may be:

* DOMESTIC SUB-CONTRACTORS, who are employed directly by the contractor.
* NOMINATED SUB-CONTRACTORS, who are proposed by the employer, usually on the architect's advice.

Nominated Sub-Contractors

A nominated sub-contractor may be selected:

* By inclusion in the Contract Bills
* In an Architect's Instruction requiring a variation.
* In the expenditure of a provisional sum.
* By agreement with the employer and contractor.

The contractor may make reasonable objection to the choice of sub-contractor, and may bid for the work himself. If successful, however, he may not sub-let the work to a domestic sub-contractor without the architect's permission.

Forms of Agreement

The 1980 Standard Form, Clauses 35.6 to 35.9, lays down procedural rules for the method of nomination (the 1991 procedure). The following forms are used:

* NSC/T - JCT Standard Form of Nominated Sub-contract Tender 1991 Edition.
* NSC/A - JCT Standard Form of Articles of Nominated Sub-contract Agreement 1991 Edition.
* NSC/C - JCT Standard Conditions of Nominated Sub-contract 1991 Edition incorporated by reference into NSC/A.
* NSC/W - JCT Standard Form of Employer/Nominated Sub-contractor Agreement 1991 Edition.
* NSC/N - JCT Standard Form of Nomination instruction.

Nomination

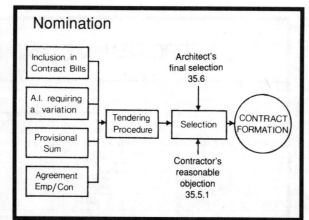

Payment

Upon issuing each interim certificate, the architect directs the contractor as to the amount due to the nominated sub-contractor. The architect must then inform the nominated sub-contractor of the amount payable. Before the issue of the next certificate, the architect must be satisfied that the nominated sub-contractor has been paid. If the contractor does not provide proof, the architect can issue a certificate to that effect which enables the employer to pay the nominated sub-contract direct and to deduct the sum from payment otherwise due to the contractor. When there are two or more nominated sub-contractors and the amount owed to the contractor is not sufficient to pay them in full, the amount available should be applied *pro rata* to all nominated sub-contractors, or some other method which the employer believes to be fair should be adopted.

Extensions

Extension to the nominated sub-contract time limits can only be effected in conformance with the sub-contract. NSC/C requires the written consent of the architect to such an extension. If the nominated sub-contractor fails to complete on time and the contractor informs the architect, he must issue a certificate to that effect (within 2 months of notification) if he is satisfied that the extension of time provisions have been carried out.

Final Payment

Clause 35.17 to 35.19 of the 1980 Standard Form regulates the final payment of nominated sub-contractors in accordance with various standard forms. In particular, it deals with the procedure where defects are found to exist in the nominated sub-contractor's work after final payment.

Nominated Suppliers

Nominated suppliers are proposed by the architect to supply goods or materials fixed by the contractor:

* Where a prime cost sum is included in the bills, and the supplier is either named in the bills, or later identified in an Architect's Instruction.
* Where a provisional sum is included in the bills which is made the subject of a prime cost sum by an Architect's Instruction in which the supplier is named.
* Where there is a provisional sum in the bills and goods for which there is a sole source of supply are specified by the architect in an Architect's Instruction.*
* Where goods for which there is a sole supplier are specified by the architect in an Architect's Instruction requiring a variation.*

* In these instances, the architect must specify a prime cost sum.

Clause 36 lays down provisions which should exist in the Contract of Sale between the contractor and the nominated supplier, e.g. payment to nominated suppliers is made by the contractor, who is allowed a 5% cash discount if he pays within 30 days of the end of the month in which the deliveries were made.

If the contractor is out of pocket as a result of obtaining goods from nominated suppliers, his expenses are added to the Contract Sum.

R
E
F

ARCHITECT'S JOB BOOK. pp. 87-90.
THE ARCHITECT"S GUIDE TO RUNNING
A JOB. pp. 67, 70-73.

1991 Procedure

- The architect sends the completed NSC/T Part 1 to the prospective sub-contractor together with a blank Part 2, the numbered tender documents and the Appendix to the main contract as it is envisaged to be completed. In addition, the architect must include a copy of NSC/W with the contract details completed.
- The sub-contractor must complete NSC/W and Part 2 of NSC/T and return them to the architect.
- The employer signs Part 2 as approved and enters into NSC/W.
- The architect then sends to the contractor a nomination instruction, NSC/N, plus NSC/T Parts 1 and 2, the numbered tender documents and NSC/W. At the same time the architect must send to the sub-contractor a copy of NSC/N, the completed NSC/W and the main contract Appendix as actually completed.
- The contractor and sub-contractor are to agree the Particular Conditions (NSC/T Part 3) and to enter into a sub-contract on NSC/A within 10 working days of receipt of NSC/N and to send the architect a copy of the completed NSC/A. If the contractor fails to enter into NSC/A he must inform the architect either:
  - The date completion of NSC/A is expected and the architect can fix such date as he thinks reasonable; or
  - That the failure is due to other matters and the architect may either:
    * Issue instructions to allow completion; or
    * Cancel nomination and omit the work; or
    * If he does not consider the matters justify the failure, notify the contractor who must enter into the contract accordingly.

Part 2 – Tender by a Sub-Contractor

Notes on completion by the Sub-Contractor

[a] Insert the same details as in NSC/T Part 1, pages 2 and 3.

In NSC/T Part 2 the expression 'Contract Administrator' is applicable where the Nomination Instruction on Nomination NSC/N will be issued under a Local Authorities version of the Standard Form of Building Contract and by a person who is not entitled to the use of the name 'Architect' under and in accordance with the Architects (Registration) Acts 1931 to 1969. If so, the expression 'Architect' shall be deemed to have been deleted throughout Tender NSC/T. Where the person who will issue the aforesaid Nomination Instruction is entitled to the use of the name 'Architect' the expression 'Contract Administrator' shall be deemed to have been deleted throughout Tender NSC/T.

To the Employer and Main Contractor

[a] Main Contract Works and location:

NEW DETACHED HOUSE
1 LETSBY AVENUE, CRINGING, WILTS

[a] Job reference: 8072

[a] Sub-Contract Works:

SWIMMING POOL

In response to the **INVITATION IN NSC/T PART 1**

We   WESMEY-SHOVELGON LTD

of (address)   2, THE BARRICADES, CRINGING, WILTS

Tel No: (010) 00001

having duly noted the information therein contained or referred to now, upon and subject to the Stipulations on page 8, OFFER for approval by or on behalf of the Employer and acceptance by the Contractor:

to carry out and complete, as a Nominated Sub-Contractor, as part of the Main Contract Works referred to in NSC/T Part 1, the Sub-Contract Works identified in the numbered tender documents listed in NSC/T Part 1 and **in accordance with all the entries we have made in this Tender (subject to agreement on items 1 to 3 with the Main Contractor when we agree the items set out in NSC/T Part 3); and**

~~to the attached further documents and~~

to complete in agreement with the Main Contractor NSC/T Part 3 (Particular Conditions), to have NSC/T Part 3 signed by us or on our behalf and to execute Agreement NSC/A (Articles of Nominated Sub-Contract Agreement) with the Main Contractor forthwith after receipt of a copy of the Nomination Instruction (Nomination NSC/N) issued to the Main Contractor under clause 35·6 of the Main Contract Conditions;

for the **VAT-exclusive Sub-Contract Sum/VAT-exclusive Tender Sum** (whichever is required by the Invitation to Tender, NSC/T Part 1, page 2) of

(words)   SIX THOUSAND FOUR HUNDRED AND TWENTY SEVEN POUNDS

£ 6,427.00

NSC/W *(left vertical margin)*

JCT

JCT Standard Form of Employer/Nominated Sub-Contractor Agreement

Agreement between a Sub-Contractor prior to being nominated for Sub-Contract Works in accordance with clauses 35·3 to 35·9 of the Standard Form of Building Contract (1980 Edition incorporating Amendments 1 to 9 and Amendment 10) and an Employer.

[a] Insert the same details as in NSC/T Part 1, pages 2 and 3.

[a] Main Contract Works ('Works') and location:

NEW DETACHED HOUSE
1, LETSBY AVENUE, CRINGING, WILTS

[a] Job reference:

8072

[a] Sub-Contract Works:

SWIMMING POOL

[b] This Agreement must be executed before the Architect/the Contract Administrator can nominate the Sub-Contractor.

[b]

This Agreement

made the 15TH day of APRIL 19 93

between HUSSEIN CHARGEER

of (or whose registered office is situated at)
1, LETSBY AVENUE, CRINGING, WILTS

(hereinafter called 'the Employer') and

WESMEY-SHOVELGON LTD

of (or whose registered office is situated at)

2, THE BARRICADES, CRINGING, WILTS

(hereinafter called 'the Sub-Contractor')

Whereas

First   the Sub-Contractor has submitted a tender on Tender NSC/T Part 2 (hereinafter called 'the Tender') on the terms and conditions in that Tender and in the Invitation to Tender NSC/T Part 1 to carry out works (as set out in the numbered tender documents enclosed therewith and referred to above and hereinafter called 'the Sub-Contract Works') as part of the Main Contract Works referred to above to be or being carried out on the terms and conditions relating thereto referred to in the Tender NSC/T Part 1 (hereinafter called 'the Main Contract'); and the Tender has been signed as 'approved' by or on behalf of the Employer;

Second   the Employer has appointed
FAIR AND SQUARE

to be the Architect/the Contract Administrator for the purposes of the Main Contract and this Agreement (hereinafter called 'the Architect/the Contract Administrator' which expression as used in this Agreement shall include his successors validly appointed under the Main Contract or otherwise if appointed before the Main Contract is operative);

Third   the Architect/the Contract Administrator on behalf of the Employer intends that after this Agreement has been executed and, if a Main Contract has not been entered into, after a Main Contract has been so entered into, to nominate the Sub-Contractor to carry out and complete the Sub-Contract Works on the terms and conditions of the Tender and the Invitation to Tender NSC/T Part 1;

continued

© 1991 RIBA Publications Ltd

JCT Standard Form of Tender by Nominated Supplier

For use in connection with the Standard Form of Building Contract (SFBC) issued by the Joint Contracts Tribunal, 1980 edition, incorporating Amendments 1 to 9

Job Title: NEW DETACHED HOUSE
(name and brief location of Works)

1, LETSBY AVENUE, CRINGING, WILTS

[a] To be completed by or on behalf of the Architect/the Contract Administrator.

Employer: [a] HUSSEIN CHARGEER

1, LETSBY AVENUE, CRINGING, WILTS

WILLIAM DURR LTD

Main Contractor: [a]
(if known)

2, THE BITTER END, CRINGING, WILTS

FITTED CARPET

Tender for: [a]
(abbreviated description)

Name of Tenderer: WALTER WALL LTD

2, THE SKIRTINGS, CRINGING, WILTS

To be returned to: [a] FAIR AND SQUARE, 4, THE HELLOVET, CRINGING, WILTS

Lump sum price: [b] £2,400.00

[b] To be completed by the supplier; see also Schedule 1, item 7.

TWO THOUSAND AND FOUR HUNDRED POUNDS *(words)*
and/or Schedule of rates (attached)

---

[c] By SFBC clause 36·4·9 none of the provisions in the contract of sale can override, modify or affect in any way the provisions incorporated from SFBC clause 36·4 in that contract of sale. Nominated Suppliers should therefore take steps to ensure that their sale conditions do not incorporate any provisions which purport to override, modify or affect in any way the provisions incorporated from SFBC clause 36·4.

1 We confirm that we will be under a contract with the Main Contractor:

·1 to supply the materials or goods described or referred to in **Schedule 1** for the price and/or at the rate set out above; and

·2 in accordance with the other terms set out in that Schedule, as a Nominated Supplier in accordance with the terms of SFBC clause 36·3 to ·5 (as set out in **Schedule 2**) and our conditions of sale in so far as they do not conflict with the terms of SFBC clause 36·3 to ·5[c]

provided:

·3 the Architect/the Contract Administrator has issued the relevant nomination instruction (a copy of which has been sent to us by the Architect/the Contract Administrator); and

·4 agreement on delivery between us and the Main Contractor has been reached as recorded in **Schedule 1** Part 6 (see SFBC clause 36·4·3); and

·5 we have thereafter received an order from the Main Contractor accepting this tender.

[d] May be completed by or on behalf of the Architect/the Contract Administrator; if not so completed, to be completed by the supplier.

2 We agree that this Tender shall be open for acceptance by an order from the Main Contractor within [d] of the date of this Tender. Provided that where the Main Contractor has not been named above we reserve the right to withdraw this Tender within 14 days of having been notified, by or on behalf of the Employer named above, of the name of the Main Contractor.

[e] To be struck out by or on behalf of the Architect/the Contract Administrator if no Warranty Agreement is required.

3[e] Subject to our right to withdraw this Tender as set out in paragraph 2 we hereby declare that we accept the Warranty Agreement in the terms set out in **Schedule 3** hereto on condition that no provision in that Warranty Agreement shall take effect unless and until

a copy to us of the instruction nominating us,
the order of the Main Contract accepting this Tender, and
a copy of the Warranty Agreement signed by the Employer

have been received by us.

For and on behalf of WALTER WALL LTD

Address 2, THE SKIRTINGS,

CRINGING, WILTS

Signature W.Wall Date 6 AUGUST 1993

Schedule 3: Warranty Agreement by a Nominated Supplier

To the Employer: HUSSEIN CHARGEER

1, LETSBY AVENUE, CRINGING, WILTS

named in our Tender dated   6 AUGUST 1993

For FITTED CARPET TO LIVING AND DINING ROOMS AND
(abbreviated description of goods/materials)

THE HALL

To be supplied to: DETACHED HOUSE
(job title)

1, LETSBY AVENUE, CRINGING, WILTS

1   Subject to the conditions stated in the above mentioned Tender (that no provision in this Warranty Agreement shall take effect unless and until the instruction nominating us, the order of the Main Contractor accepting the Tender and a copy of this Warranty Agreement signed by the Employer have been received by us) WE WARRANT in consideration of our being nominated in respect of the supply of the goods and/or materials to be supplied by us as a Nominated Supplier under the Standard Form of Building Contract referred to in the Tender and in accordance with the description, quantity and quality of the materials or goods and with the other terms and details set out in the Tender ('the supply') that:

1·1   We have exercised and will exercise all reasonable skill and care in:

1·1   ·1   the design of the supply insofar as the supply has been or will be designed by us; and

·2   the selection of materials and goods for the supply insofar as such supply has been or will be selected by us; and

·3   the satisfaction of any performance specification or requirement insofar as such performance specification or requirement is included or referred to in the Tender as part of the description of the supply.

1·2   We will:

1·2   ·1   save insofar as we are delayed by:

·1   force majeure; or

·2   civil commotion, local combination of workmen, strike or lock-out; or

·3   any instruction of the Architect/the Contract Administrator under SFBC clause 13·2 (Variations) or clause 13·3 (provisional sums); or

Pages 1 to 6 comprising Tender and Schedules 1 and 2 are issued in a separate pad, TNS/1 (SFBC).

© 1991 RIBA Publications Ltd

Page 7

1·2   ·1   continued

·4   failure of the Architect/the Contract Administrator to supply to us within due time any necessary information for which we have specifically applied in writing on a date which was neither unreasonably distant from nor unreasonably close to the date on which it was necessary for us to receive the same

so supply the Architect/the Contract Administrator with such information as the Architect the Contract Administrator may reasonably require; and

·2   so supply the Contractor with such information as the Contractor may reasonably require in accordance with the arrangements in our contract of sale with the Contractor; and

·3   so commence and complete delivery of the supply in accordance with the arrangements in our contract of sale with the Contractor

that the Contractor shall not become entitled to an extension of time under SFBC clauses 25·4·6 or 25·4·7 of the Main Contract Conditions nor become entitled to be paid for direct loss and or expense ascertained under SFBC clause 26·1 for the matters referred to in clause 26·2·1 of the Main Contract Conditions; and we will indemnify you to the extent but not further or otherwise that the Architect/the Contract Administrator is obliged to give an extension of time so that the Employer is unable to recover damages under the Main Contract for delays in completion, and or pay an amount in respect of direct loss and/or expense as aforesaid because of any failure by us under clause 1·2·1 or 1·2·2 hereof.

2   We have noted the amount of the liquidated and ascertained damages under the Main Contract, as stated in TNS/1 Schedule 1, item 8.

3   Nothing in the Tender is intended to or shall exclude or limit our liability for breach of the warranties set out above.

4·1   In case any dispute or difference shall arise between the Employer or the Architect the Contract Administrator on his behalf and ourselves as to the construction of this Agreement or as to any matter or thing of whatsoever nature arising out of this Agreement or in connection therewith then such dispute or difference shall be and is hereby referred to arbitration. When we or the Employer require such dispute or difference to be referred to arbitration we or the Employer shall given written notice to the other to such effect and such dispute or difference shall be referred to the arbitration and final decision of a person to be agreed between the parties as the Arbitrator, or, upon failure so to agree within 14 days after the date of the aforesaid written notice, of a person to be appointed as the Arbitrator on the request of either ourselves or the Employer by the person named in the Appendix to the Standard Form of Building Contract referred to in the Tender.

4·2   ·1   Provided that if the dispute or difference to be referred to arbitration under this Agreement raises issues which are substantially the same as or connected with the issues raised in a related dispute between the Employer and the Contractor under the Main Contract or between a Nominated Sub-Contractor and the Contractor under Sub-Contract NSC 4 or NSC/4a or between the Employer and any other Nominated Supplier, and if the related dispute has also been referred for determination to an Arbitrator, the Employer and ourselves hereby agree that the dispute or difference under this Agreement shall be referred to the Arbitrator appointed to determine the related dispute; and the JCT Arbitration Rules applicable to the related dispute shall apply to the dispute under this Agreement; and such Arbitrator shall have power to make such directions and all necessary awards in the same way as if the procedure of the High Court as to joining one or more of the defendants or joining co-defendants or third parties was available to the parties and to him; and the agreement of consent referred to in paragraph 4·6 on appeals or applications to the High Court on any question of law shall apply to any question of law arising out of the awards of such Arbitrator in respect of all related disputes referred to him or arising in the course of the reference of all the related disputes referred to him.

·2   Save that the Employer or ourselves may require the dispute or difference under this Agreement to be referred to a different Arbitrator (to be appointed under this Agreement) if either of us reasonably considers that the Arbitrator appointed to determine the related dispute is not properly qualified to determine the dispute or difference under this Agreement.

·3   Paragraphs 4·2·1 and 4·2·2 hereof shall apply unless in the Appendix to the Standard Form of Building Contract referred to in the Tender the words 'clause 41·2·1 and 41·2·2 apply' have been deleted.

© 1991 RIBA Publications Ltd

Page 8

4·3   Such reference shall not be opened until after Practical Completion or alleged Practical Completion of the Main Contract Works or termination or alleged termination of the Contractor's employment under the Main Contract or abandonment of the Main Contract Works, unless with the written consent of the Employer or the Architect/the Contract Administrator on his behalf and ourselves.

4·4   Subject to paragraph 4·5 the award of such Arbitrator shall be final and binding on the parties.

4·5   The parties hereby agree and consent pursuant to Sections 1(3) and 2(1) (b) of the Arbitration Act, 1979, that either party

·1   may appeal to the High Court on any question of law arising out of an award made in any arbitration under this Arbitration Agreement; and

·2   may apply to the High Court to determine any question of law arising in the course of the reference;

and the parties agree that the High Court should have jurisdiction to determine any such question of law.

4·6   Whatever the nationality, residence or domicile of ourselves or the Employer, the Contractor, any sub-contractor or supplier or the Arbitrator, and wherever the Works or any part thereof are situated, the law of England shall be the proper law of this Warranty and in particular (but not so as to derogate from the generality of the foregoing) the provisions of the Arbitration Acts 1950 (notwithstanding anything in S.34 thereof) to 1979 shall apply to any arbitration under this Contract wherever the same, or any part of it, shall be conducted.[*]

4·7   If before his final award the Arbitrator dies or otherwise ceases to act as the Arbitrator, the Employer and ourselves shall forthwith appoint a further Arbitrator, or, upon failure so to appoint within 14 days of any such death or cessation, then either the Employer or ourselves may request the person named in the Appendix to the Standard Form of Building Contract referred to in the Tender to appoint such further Arbitrator. Provided that no such further Arbitrator shall be entitled to disregard any direction of the previous Arbitrator or to vary or revise any award of the previous Arbitrator except to the extent that the previous Arbitrator had power so to do under the JCT Arbitration Rules and/or with the agreement of the parties and/or by the operation of law.

4·8   The arbitration shall be conducted in accordance with the 'JCT Arbitration Rules' current at the date of the Tender. Provided that if any amendments to the Rules so current have been issued by the Joint Contracts Tribunal after the aforesaid date the Employer and Supplier may, by a joint notice in writing to the Arbitrator, state that they wish the arbitration to be conducted in accordance with the JCT Arbitration Rules as so amended.[†]

[††]Signature of or on behalf of the Supplier: W. Wall

[††]Signature of or on behalf of the Employer: H Chargeer

[*]Where the parties do not wish the proper law of the Warranty to be the law of England appropriate amendments to paragraph 4·7 should be made. Where the Works are situated in Scotland then the forms issued by the Scottish Building Contract Committee which contain Scots proper law and arbitration provisions are the appropriate documents. It should be noted that the provisions of the Arbitration Acts 1950 to 1979 do not apply to arbitrations conducted in Scotland.

[†] The JCT Arbitration Rules contain stricter time limits than those prescribed by some arbitration rules or those frequently observed in practice. The parties should note that a failure by a party or the agent of a party to comply with the time limits incorporated in these Rules may have adverse consequences.

[††] If the Warranty Agreement is to be executed as a deed advice should be sought on the correct method of execution.

© 1991 RIBA Publications Ltd

Page 9

TELEPHONE MESSAGE

Date 8.OCT.94

~~ame~~ 10.30.a.m.

From Arthur Bitter   To Bill F.
      (builder)

Concerning

Tenders for the Council job.

He says he has discovered a substantial
error in his bid, which was accepted
yesterday. Can he change it?

Taken By V.N.

1, Forthey Road
Cringing
Wilts

Dear Mr Square,   October 16th

        Regarding the project in the neighbouring
plot at 2, Forthey Road; I have been through the
Standard Form of Building Contract (Private with
Quantities) which you suggested we use, and find I
am not satisfied with several of the conditions.

        I enclose a revised copy containing amendments
and additions which I have made. I think we should
use this instead.

        Yours truly,

        O. fforagh-Nuther
        O. fforagh-Nuther

MEMO

To   : TOM SQUARE

From   : ROY TRING

Date   : OCT.19.

Concerning : TYPE OF CONTRACT

WE'VE BEEN ASKED TO DEAL WITH THE RENOVATION OF
A DILAPIDATED COACH-HOUSE. THE OWNER WANTS TO
CONVERT IT INTO A RESTAURANT/PRIVATE CLUB, AND
WANTS TO OPEN AS SOON AS POSSIBLE - WHAT SORT OF
CONTRACT SHOULD WE ADVISE?

                                R.T.

DESK DIARY

OCT 19

re: Bitter's errors.
Contractually, the agreement is binding but in the Selective Tendering Code, errors are dealt with in this case under Alternative I, so that the employer could have allowed a change, but too late now. Anyway, not our problem; Inform the Council & wait for instructions before proceeding.

OCT 20

re: fforagh-Nither's alterations to Standard Form.
Write & dissuade — Fiddling with the standard clauses is asking for trouble.

OCT 21

re: Coach-house renovation
Suggest Cost + Fluctuating fee contract.
The work will be tricky and its unlikely that we can get an accurate price at the outset. The Fluctuating fee will a) help to keep the cost down.
b) Make sure the work's done as fast as possible.

Fair and Square

CHARTERED ARCHITECTS

B.FAIR.dip.arch.RIBA.
T.SQUARE.B.Arch.RIBA.AFAS.

BF/vn

4, The Hellovet,
Cringing,
Wilts.

22.10.94

Dear Mr fforagh-Nuther,

Re : Proposed House at 2 Forthey Road

Thank you for your letter of the 16th October. With regard to the amendments you propose, we would strongly advise that you consider the consequences of such an action. The Standard Form is a complex, comprehensive document containing many inter-dependent conditions. They have been drafted under expert guidance, based on detailed knowledge of the construction process, and any interference with the accepted format may lead to incalculable consequences later in the project.

The changes you propose do not seem to merit the problems they may cause, and we would not really be happy to proceed, at least until professional legal advice has been taken. May we suggest that, if you are convinced that the Standard Form is inadequate, it would be to our mutual benefit if you sought legal assistance in this matter.

We look forward to hearing from you,

Yours sincerely,

Fair & Square

Fair and Square.

O. fforagh-Nuther
1 Forthey Road
Cringing
Wilts

SECTION SIX

THE CONSTRUCTION PHASE

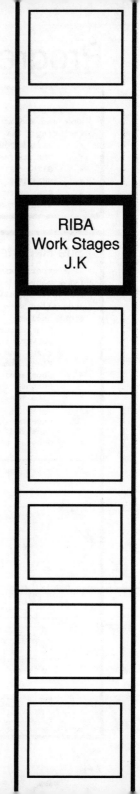

RIBA
Work Stages
J.K

Progress Appraisal

The progress of operations on site may be assessed and monitored by a number of mechanisms including:
- **SITE REPORTS**
- **THE CONTRACTOR'S PROGRAMME**
- **SITE VISITS**
- **MEETINGS**
- **EXPENDITURE FORECAST COMPARED WITH ACTUAL CERTIFICATION**

Site Reports

Site reports are written by the clerk of works (if employed) or the site supervisor, and submitted weekly to the architect, constituting a detailed record of the job. The site report might include:
- **Contractor's workforce per day**
- **Sub-contractor's workforce per day**
- **Plant and materials delivered to the site**
- **Plant removed from the site**
- **Shortages, stoppages and delays**
- **Weather report and temperature details**
- **Site visitors and meetings**
- **Dates of information required and drawings, Architect's Instructions etc. received**
- **General progress and observations**

CLERK OF WORKS REPORT

CONTRACT _____   CONTRACTOR _____
CLERK of WORKS _____

1 PROGRESS			week ending											3 SITE REPORT	week ending
element	date	10	20	30	40	50	60	70	80	90	comp.				

2 LABOUR RETURN																4 SITE RECORD			
Main Contractor							Sub-Contractor								AInos drawings		Visitors during week	
	m	t	w	th	f	s	su	m	t	w	th	f	s	su				

time lost | m | t | w | th | f | s | su | week | to date |

	mon	tues	wed	thur	fri	sat	sun
wea.							
temp.							

total ___   total ___

The Programme

The contractor's programme (see p 65), can be used as a means of assessing the contractor's performance in relation to his original estimates and intentions, and in relation to the site reports. This is particularly easy if the programme is computerised.

Site Visits

Site visits are dealt with on p 78.

Meetings

Meetings may be held periodically between various parties during the construction process. types of meetings include:
- **PROJECT MEETINGS, for architectural staff to discuss the particular project**
- **CONTRACTOR MEETINGS, held between the contractor and sub-contractors (and the architect may attend if asked), preferably just prior to the**
- **MAIN SITE MEETINGS, which may be held:**
  - **At regular intervals**
  - **At specific times in the construction process**
  - **When problems occur**
  - **When it seems necessary to provide impetus**

Those attending, in addition to the architect and the contractor may include:
- **The employer**
- **The user**
- **The clerk of works**
- **The quantity surveyor**
- **Various consultants**

Procedure

Whoever takes responsibility for chairing a site meeting (usually the architect) will prepare and distribute the minutes not more than 7 days after the event. Dissents should be registered immediately.

All parties due to attend should be notified 7 days prior to the proposed meeting unless the date has already been fixed at the previous meeting.

The Agenda

At the meeting:
- **Take the names of those present.**
- **Give the names of those sending apologies. AGENDA:**
- **Agree minutes of the last meeting, or deal with any problems arising from them.**
- **Contractor's report.**
- **Clerk of works' report (if employed).**
- **Consultants' reports.**
- **Quantity surveyor's report.**
- **Communications and procedures: any action required, by whom, etc.**
- **Contract progress.**
- **Any other business.**
- **Time and place of next meeting.**

AGENDA

JOB TITLE : _____   JOB CODE : ___

PROGRESS MEETING No : _____

1. Agreement to minutes of Meeting No... held on . . .
2. Matters arising.
3. Progress to date.
   3.1 Contractors
   3.2 Clerk of Works
   3.3 Consultants
   3.4 Q.S.
4. Matters affecting progress.
5. Any other business.
6. Date of next meeting.

DISTRIBUTION :

Employer	I	Elec. Con.	I
Contractor	I	Structural Con.	I
Q S	I	Clerk of Works	I
Mech. Con.	I	File	I

REF ARCHITECT'S JOB BOOK. pp. 103-115.
ARCHITECT'S GUIDE TO RUNNING A JOB. pp. 112-119.

Variations

Contract Variations

Despite the preparation of detailed drawings and bills, it is possible that the quality or the quantity of the proposed work agreed upon in the contract documents will need to be changed. Contractually, the contractor need do nothing that is not agreed upon, and so the contract (Standard Form) contains a provision allowing for additions, alterations and omissions from the originally proposed work.
the need for a variation may stem from:
* Inadequate design work
* Changes of mind or opinion after the contract has been signed
* Unforeseen circumstances

Definition

A variation has only limited scope and cannot, for example, be used to change the essence of the contract. If such a fundamental change was required, it would be necessary to determine the contract by mutual consent, and draft a new one. A variation is an "alteration or modification of the design, quality or quantity of the Works as shown upon the Contract Drawings and described by or referred to in the Contract Bills" (Standard Form Clause 13.1.1.), or the imposition, variation or omission of restrictions (Standard form clause 13.1.2.). Dependent upon the characteristics of the change required, it may be difficult to determine whether a variation is necessary. For example, if the job cost more than the contractor expected, this would not be grounds for a variation (although it would probably be dealt with under a fluctuations clause).

Authorisation

If the work qualifies for a variation, a written order is required to justify payment. For this purpose, it is advisable to use an Architect's Instruction (see page 77). The architect's signature must always appear by way of authorisation. If the clerk of works issues an authorisation, it is of no effect unless confirmed by the architect in writing within 2 days.

Cost

The cost of the variation may be calculated by:
* An agreed price
* Measurement and valuation by a quantity surveyor
* Reference to the Contract Bill rates, varied if necessary to suit changes in conditions
* Daywork basis plus percentage additions in accordance with definitions set out in the Contract Documents
* A fair valuation

Effects

Authorisation of a variation may result in:
Increased cost to the client
Increased time necessary to complete
which may affect:
* Insurances
* bonuses
* hire charges
* extra fees (architect, clerk of works)
* other expenditure or financial loss (e.g. loss of potential rent, moving expenses etc.)
in which case the employer must be informed, and the quantity surveyor notified to assess the situation and its consequences.

Provisions

Variations are often provided for in:
* PROVISIONAL SUMS in the contract. These are sums provided for work or for costs which cannot be entirely foreseen e.g. for work of an experimental nature.
* PRIME COST SUMS i.e. sums of money included in the contract to be expended on materials from suppliers or work carried out by Nominated Sub-Contractors.
It is possible for a provisional sum to become a prime cost sum upon the issuance of an Architect's Instruction to that effect.

The Architect's Instruction

The RIBA produce a standard ARchitect's Instruction form which may conveniently be used for a number of matters including:
* Errors in Bills of Quantities (c.2.2.2.2)
* Discrepancies between the Contract Drawings and the Bills of Quantities (c.2.3)
* Statutory obligations (c.6.1.3)
* Errors in setting out not to be amended and adjustment to Contract Sum (c.7)
* Opening up, inspection and testing (c.8.3)
* Removal of materials and goods not in accordance with the Contract (c.8.4)
* Variations after discovery of defective work (c.8.4.3)
* Opening up, inspection and testing after discovery of defective work (c.8.4.4)
* Variations or opening up if work not carried out in workmanlike manner
* Exclusion of persons from the works (c.8.6)
* Confirmation of a clerk of works' direction (c.12)
* Requirement or sanction of variations (c.13.2)
* Expenditure of provisional sums included in the Contract Bills (c.13.3.1)
* Expenditure of provisional sums included in a sub-contract (c.13.3.2)
* To sanction the removal of unfixed materials and goods from site (c.16.1)
* Schedule of defects (c.17.2)
* Requirement that defects be made good within the Defects Liability Period or that they are not to be made good, and an appropriate adjustment be made to the Contract Sum (c.17.3)
* Postponement of work (c.23.2)
* Discovery of antiquities (c.34.2)
* To remove objection to Sub-contractor (c.35.5.2)
* To omit work of sub-contractor or to require selection of another sub-contractor (c.35.23)
* To require contractor to give sub-contractor notice specifying the relevant default (c.35.24.6.1)
* To nominate suppliers (c.36.2)

REF THE ARCHITECT'S GUIDE TO RUNNING A JOB. pp. 120-121.
THE ARCHITECT IN PRACTICE. pp. 197-207.

Architect/CA: FAIR & SQUARE
address: 4, THE HELLOVET, CRINGING, WILTS

Employer: HUSSEIN CHARGEER
address: 1, LETSBY AVENUE, CRINGING, WILTS.

Contractor: WILLIAM DURR LTD
address: 2, THE BITTER END, CRINGING, WILTS

Works: NEW DETACHED HOUSE
situated at: 1, LETSBY AVENUE, CRINGING, WILTS

Contract dated: 29 JAN 1993

Clerk of Works Direction

Job reference: 8072

Direction no: 5

Issue date: 7 JULY 1993

Original to Contractor

Under the terms of the above-mentioned Contract, I issue the following direction.

This direction shall be of no effect unless confirmed in writing by the Architect/the Contract Administrator within 2 working days, and does not authorise any extra payment.

Direction	Architect/CA use
1. PLASTERBOARD NOT STORED & PROTECTED AFTER DELIVERY, AND HAS BECOME DAMAGED BY RAIN. THIS IS TO BE REMOVED AND REPLACED.	
2. FAIRFACED PRECAST DOOR CILLS ARE BADLY CRACKED AND CHIPPED. CAREFULLY REMOVE AND REPLACE	

Signed I. Sawyer   Clerk of Works

Covered by Instruction no:

F810 for JCT 80   © RIBA Publications Ltd 1991

Issued by: FAIR AND SQUARE
address: 4, THE HELLOVET, CRINGING, WILTS

Architect's Instruction

Employer: HUSSEIN CHARGEER
address: 1, LETSBY AVENUE, CRINGING, WILTS

Job reference: 8072

Instruction no: 18

Contractor: WILLIAM DURR LTD
address: 2, THE BITTER END, CRINGING, WILTS

Issue date: 8 July 1993

Sheet: of

Works: NEW DETACHED HOUSE
situated at: 1, LETSBY AVENUE, CRINGING, WILTS

Contract dated: 29 January 1993

Under the terms of the above-mentioned Contract, I/we issue the following instructions:

	Office use: Approx costs	
	£ omit	£ add
1. We confirm the issue of the Clerk of Works Direction No. 5 dated 7 July 1993.		
2. We confirm our oral instruction to you on 6 July 1993, to take down and remove from the site the screen wall, which was not built in accordance with the drawings and specification, and rebuild. This work is to be carried out at your own expense.		

To be signed by or for
the issuer named
above

Signed _Fair & Square_

Amount of Contract Sum £
± Approximate value of previous Instructions £

± Approximate value of this Instruction £
Approximate adjusted total £

Distribution

Original to:
☐1 Contractor

Copies to:
☐1 Employer
☐1 Nominated Sub-Contractors
☐1 Quantity Surveyor
☐ Consultants
☐1 Clerk of Works
☐1 File

F809 for JCT 80/IFC 84/MW 80   © RIBA Publications Ltd 1991

The Architect's Duties

Although not a party to the building contract, the architect, in his role of agent, has several duties to perform in the construction process. The designated powers which create these duties are stated in the Conditions of the Standard Form (over 50 exist), and care should be taken not to exceed jurisdiction by doing anything which, although seemingly relevant, forms no part of the architect's actual duties. For example, if asked for advice on how to build a part of the project, the architect should decline, remembering that it is the contractor's contractual obligation to ensure compliance with contract documents.

The architect's duties cover two principal areas :   PERFORMANCE EVALUATION
                CERTIFICATION

Performance Evaluation

In evaluating the contractor's performance, the architect plays 2 distinct roles:
- INSPECTOR: Where so required by the contract, the architect must check that certain work is in absolute accordance with the contract documents.
- JUDGE: Other clauses of the Standard Form require the architect to provide a qualitative opinion on work. The clauses imposing this duty are phrased "to the architect's satisfaction".

In order that these duties may be fulfilled, certain powers are granted to the architect by the Standard Form including:

- The ordering of tests to be made on goods, materials or workmanship.
- The requiring of proof of compliance of goods or materials with the contract documents.
- The ordering of work to be uncovered for testing.
- The ordering of work that is not in accordance with the contract to be removed.
- The ordering of any person on site who is not working to the architect's satisfaction to be removed.

Certification (see p 60).

At prescribed stages in the construction programme, the architect is empowered to check the work completed to date and, if he finds it to be in accordance with the contract and to his satisfaction, the value of the work is calculated (frequently by the quantity surveyor). The architect must then issue an Interim Certificate (see p 79), to be sent to the employer, with copies for the quantity surveyor, the contractor and the file.The employer is obliged to pay the certified amount within 14 days. At the same time, the architect sends a Notification to the sub-contractors indicating the issuance of the certificate, and directions to the contractor to pay the sub-contractors the relevant amount.

Prior to 1974, the architect had a quasi-arbitral immunity in respect of claims arising out of his negligent certification (see p.10). Since the removal of this protection, great care should be exercised before issuing any certificate and the quantity surveyor should be given a list of defective work each month with instructions to omit such work from the valuation.

Site Visits

Periodical site visits should be made by the architect, and the intervals will depend upon a number of factors including:

- Type and complexity of the project.
- Nature of the employer.
- Personal knowledge of the contractor.
- Locality of the site.
- Whether or not a clerk of works is employed.
- Particular events, for example, the arrival of equipment.
- Unforeseen events, for example, bad weather.
- The stage of the work reached.

On arrival, the architect should inform the person-in-charge of his presence, and remember only to deal with him (or his representative) during the visit. A record should be kept of all site visits, noting any observations, information supplied, and actions to be taken. A copy of the record may then be sent to the quantity surveyor.

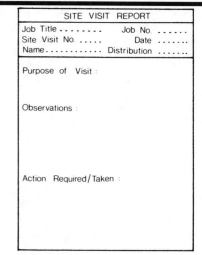

SITE VISIT REPORT

Job Title .... Job No. .....
Site Visit No. ..... Date .....
Name........... Distribution .....

Purpose of Visit :

Observations :

Action Required/Taken :

Visits might arise out of the following:
- Positioning of site huts.
- Establishment of datum points, bench marks and building layout.
- Dimensions and grades.
- Safety and security provisions.
- Protection of trees etc.
- Fences, hoardings, signs etc.
- Siting of spoil heaps.
- Excavations and soil underfootings.
- Testing of drainage.
- Public utility connections.
- Foundations, reinforcement, pile driving, caissons.
- Concrete tests, formwork, reinforcement.
- Structural frames.
- Floor openings, sleeves and hangers.
- Quality and placing of concrete.
- Weather precautions.
- Masonry layout, materials.
- Bonding and flashing.
- Frames and prefabricated elements.
- Partition layout.
- Temporary enclosures, heat and light.
- Protection of finished work.
- Partitions and plasterwork.
- Tiles, electrical work and wiring.

R
E
F

ARCHITECT'S JOB BOOK. pp. 119-121.
PRACTICE MANAGEMENT
HANDBOOK. pp. 295-298.
THE ARCHITECT'S GUIDE TO RUNNING
A JOB. pp. 128-135.

Issued by: FAIR AND SQUARE
address: 4, THE HELLOVET, CRINGING, WILTS

Employer: HUSSEIN CHARGEER
address: 1, LETSBY AVENUE, CRINGING, WILTS

Contractor: WILLIAM DURR LTD
address: 2, THE BITTER END, CRINGING, WILTS

Works: NEW DETACHED HOUSE
situated at: 1, LETSBY AVENUE, CRINGING, WILTS

Contract dated: 29 January 1993

Interim Certificate and Direction

Serial no: **C 449613**

Job reference: 8072

Certificate no: 8

Issue date: 8 October 1993

Valuation date: 1 October 1993

Contract sum: £156,000.00

Original to Employer

This Interim Certificate is issued under the terms of the above-mentioned Contract.

Gross valuation inclusive of the value of works by Nominated Sub-Contractors .... £ 138,000.00

Less Retention which may be retained by the Employer as detailed on the Statement of Retention .... £ 6,900.00

Sub-total £ 131,100.00

Less total amount stated as due in Interim Certificates previously issued up to and including Interim Certificate no: 7 .... £ 120,000.00

Net amount for payment .... £ 11,100.00

I/We hereby certify that the **amount for payment** by the Employer to the Contractor on this Certificate is (in words)

Eleven thousand one hundred pounds only.

I/We hereby direct the Contractor that this amount includes interim or final payments to Nominated Sub-Contractors as listed in the attached *Statement of Retention and of Nominated Sub-Contractors' Values*, which are to be discharged to those named in accordance with the Sub-Contract.

All amounts are exclusive of VAT

To be signed by or for the issuer named above

Signed *Fair & Square*

[1] Relevant only if clause 1A of the VAT Agreement applies. Delete if not applicable.

[t] The Contractor has given notice that the rate of VAT chargeable on the supply of goods and services to which the Contract relates is %

[1] % of the amount certified above is .... £

[1] Total of net amount and VAT amount (for information) .... £

This is not a Tax Invoice

Issued by: FAIR AND SQUARE
address: 4, THE HELLOVET, CRINGING, WILTS

Employer: HUSSEIN CHARGEER
address: 1, LETSBY AVENUE, CRINGING, WILTS

Job reference: 8072

Notification no: 2

Main Contractor: WILLIAM DURR LTD
address: 2, THE BITTER END, CRINGING, WILTS

Issue date: 8 October 1993

Works: NEW DETACHED HOUSE
situated at: 1, LETSBY AVENUE, CRINGING, WILTS

Contract dated: 29 January 1993

Original to Nominated Sub-Contractor

Nominated WESMEY-SHOVELGON LTD
Sub-Contractor:
address: 2, THE BARRICADES, CRINGING, WILTS

Under the terms of the above-mentioned Main Contract,

I/we hereby inform you that we have directed the Contractor that

Interim Certificate no.　8　dated　8 October 1993

*Delete as appropriate

includes *an interim/x final payment of £1,850.00
which is to be discharged to you.

A copy of a statement of retention is attached.

To be signed by or for the issuer named above

Signed _Fair & Square_

- -

Main Contractor: WILLIAM DURR LTD
address: 2, THE BITTER END, CRINGING, WILTS

Nominated Sub-Contractor's
**Acknowledgement
of Discharge**
of payment due

Works: NEW DETACHED HOUSE
situated at: 1, LETSBY AVENUE, CRINGING, WILTS

Job reference: 8072

In accordance with the terms of the relevant Sub-Contract,
we confirm that we have received from you discharge of the amount of ..... £ 1,850.00

included in Interim Certificate no.　8　dated　8 October 1993

as stated in Notification no.　2　dated　8 October 1993

Please complete acknowledgement slip and send to Contractor

Signed _W. Wm_　　Date 22·10·93

For　Wesmey-Shovelgon Ltd

F803 for JCT 80

© RIBA Publications Ltd 1991

Statement of Retention

Statement of Retention
and of Nominated Sub-Contractors' Values

Issued by:
address: FAIR AND SQUARE
4, THE HELLOVET, CRINGING, WILTS

Works: NEW DETACHED HOUSE

situated at: 1, LETSBY AVENUE, CRINGING, WILTS

Job reference: 8072
Relating to Certificate no: 8
Issue date: 8 October 1993

	Gross valuation	Amount subject to:				Amount of retention	Net valuation	Previously certified	Balance due
		Full retention of 5 %	Half retention %	Nil retention				
	£	£	£	£		£	£	£	£
Main Contractor									
WILLIAM DURR LTD	135,000	135,000	–	–		6,750	128,250	119,000	9,250
Nominated Sub-Contractors:									
WESMEY-SHOVELGON LTD	3,000	3,000	–	–		150	2,850	1,000	1,850
Total	138,000	138,000	–	–		6,900	131,100	120,000	11,100

All amounts are exclusive of VAT

No account has been taken of any discounts for cash to which the Contractor may be entitled if discharging the balance within 17 days of the issue of the Interim Certificate.

F802   for JCT 80

We are grateful to the Royal Institution of Chartered Surveyors for allowing us to adapt their copyright form of the same title.
© RIBA Publications 1992

81

Delays

Dealing with Delays

Building contracts generally stipulate a completion date in the Appendix. If the contractor does not finish within the time allocated, he is in breach of the Contract. Several mechanisms exist in the 1980 Standard Form of Building Contract (JCT - Private with Quantities) to deal with delays:

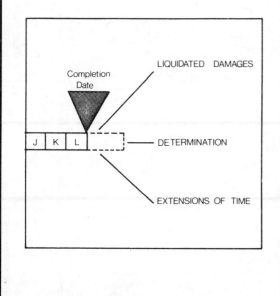

Liquidated Damages (Clause 24)

These are specified in the Appendix, and provide for an agreed sum to be paid by the contractor for every day or week that completion is overdue.

Determination

In certain circumstances, the contractor's employment under the contract may be determined (see page 96).

Extensions of time (Clause 25)

Should the date for completion be delayed by virtue of an agreed clause, the contract time may be extended accordingly. Examples of events which might entail an extension of time include:

• Force majeure
• Deferment of possession
• Exceptionally adverse weather conditions
• Loss or damage by specified perils
• Civil commotion, strikes etc.
• Compliance with certain Architect's
Instructions: • Discrepancies 2.3.
               • Variations 13.2.
               • Provisional sums 13.3.
               • Postponement 23.3.
               • Antiquities 34.
               • Nominated sub-contractors 35.
               • Nominated suppliers 36.
               • Opening up 8.3.
• Requested information not received in time
• Delay by a nominated sub-contractor or nominated supplier (provided that the contractor has made every practicable effort to reduce such delay)
• Work or materials which the employer has supplied or failed to supply
• Exercise of statutory powers by Government.
• Effects of statutory obligations.
• Unforeseen labour shortages or material shortages.
• Employer's failure to give necessary access to and from the site
• Approximate quantities not reasonably accurate forecast

It is the duty of the contractor to use his 'best endeavours' to prevent any delay, but if the delay is inevitable, then in order to be entitled to an extension of time, the contractor must:

• Give a written notice to the architect whenever a delay occurs or is expected, stating the cause and specifying the Relevant Event (as listed above) if appropriate.

• Where a nominated sub-contractor is involved, he should receive a copy of the notice.

• The expected effects of any Relevant Event must be detailed (either in the notice or as soon as possible afterwards) with an estimated delay time.

• Any changes in circumstances or estimates should also be notified.

Note that every delay must be notified, even those which are clearly the fault of the contractor.

The architect will then assess the notification, requiring such proof as he feels necessary (e.g. claims due to adverse weather may need to be supported by meteorological reports), and make a 'fair and reasonable' decision. The architect should notify the contractor of the new completion date stating which Relevant Events he has taken into account. The new date must be fixed not later than 12 weeks from receipt of the request or, on a project with less than 12 weeks left to the original completion date, not later than that original date. Nominated sub-contractors should also be notified in writing of any architect's decision with regard to the completion date, and the contractor must be notified if no extension is to be granted. At any time after the Contract Completion Date, but not later than 12 weeks **after** Practical Completion, the architect must review the situation and issue a notice:

• Fixing a new date for Completion
• Confirming the existing date even if no notification has been received.

Specified Perils

• Fire
• Lightning
• Explosion
• Storm
• Tempest
• Flood
• Bursting or overflowing of water tanks, apparatus or pipes
• Earthquake
• Aircraft and other aerial devices or articles dropped therefrom
• Riot and civil commotion

Excluding any loss or damaged caused by:

• Ionising radiations
• Contamination by radioactivity from any nuclear fuel or from any nuclear waste from the combustion of nuclear fuel, radioactive toxic explosive or other hazardous properties of any explosive nuclear assembly or nuclear component thereof
• Pressure waves caused by aircraft or other aerial devices travelling at sonic or supersonic speeds.

R
E
F

THE ARCHITECT IN PRACTICE. pp. 224-227.
THE ARCHITECT'S GUIDE TO RUNNING
A JOB. pp. 78-79.

Notification of
Revision to

**Completion
Date**

Issued by: FAIR AND SQUARE
address: 4, THE HELLOVET, CRINGING, WILTS

Employer: HUSSEIN CHARGEER
address: 1, LETSBY AVENUE, CRINGING, WILTS

Job reference: 8072

Notification no: 1

Contractor: WILLIAM DURR LTD
address: 2, THE BITTER END, CRINGING, WILTS

Issue date: 26 April 1993

Works: NEW DETACHED HOUSE
situated at: 1, LETSBY AVENUE, CRINGING, WILTS

Contract dated: 29 January 1993

Under the terms of the above-mentioned Contract,

A. I/we give notice that the Completion Date for

*Delete as
appropriate

*1. the Works
*2. ~~Section No xxxxxxxxxxx of the Works~~ _____

previously fixed as

17 December _____ 19 93 _____

*3. is hereby fixed later than that previously fixed,
*4. ~~is hereby fixed earlier than that previously fixed~~
*5. ~~is hereby confirmed~~

and is now

24 December _____ 19 93 _____

B. *1. This revision has taken into account the following Relevant
Events:
25.4.2 Exceptionally adverse weather 1 week
as on Contractor's notice of 18 March 1993

*2. ~~This revision has taken into account the omission of work required
by the following Instructions:~~
~~xxxxxxxxxxxxxxxxxxxxxxxx~~

*3. ~~This revision is made by reason of my/our review pursuant to
clause 25.3.3.~~
~~xxxxxxxxx~~

To be signed by or for
the issuer named
above

Signed _Fair & Square_ _____

Distribution	Original to:	Copies to:		
	☐1 Contractor	☐1 Employer	☐1 Quantity Surveyor	☐1 Clerk of Works
		☐1 Nominated Sub-Contractors	☐1 Consultants	☐1 File

F808 for JCT 80

© RIBA Publications Ltd 1990

Fair and Square

CHARTERED ARCHITECTS

B.FAIR.dip.arch.RIBA.
T.SQUARE.B.Arch.RIBA.AFAS.

4, The Hellovet,
Cringing,
Wilts.

BF/vn   11.8.94

Dear Mr Durr,

       re: Development at Letsby Avenue, Cringing.

On behalf of the owner of the above property, Mr Hussein Chargeer,
I am confirming that he took possession of the garage and
detached workshop in accordance with Clause 18 of the Standard
Form of Contract on August 9th 1994.

      Yours sincerely,

      Fair & Square.

      Fair and Square.

William Durr Esq,
2, The Bitter End,
Cringing,
Wilts.

On some projects, it is possible that a part
or portion of the works may be capable of
occupancy by the owner prior to completion of
the whole project. In this case, a 'written
statement' is sent by the architect to the
contractor confirming the date of possession
and identifying the part of the work in
question. It is also advisable for the
architect to remind the owner of the transfer
of insurance responsibilities for the
occupied portion.

TELEPHONE MESSAGE

Date NOV.15.

3.30.p.m.

To BF/TS

H.CHARGEER

concerning

CHARGEER VISITED THE SITE
YESTERDAY, AND WANTS A) A BAY
WINDOW ADDED TO THE BEDROOM AND
B) AN EXTRA
WING ON THE BACK TO HOUSE A BILLIARD
ROOM ETC.

WILL YOU DEAL WITH THIS FOR HIM?

Taken By V.N.

WESMEY–SHOVELGON LTD

Dear Messrs. Fair and Square,

I am writing to you in connection with the job in Letsby Avenue, where we are working as Nominated Sub-Contractors.

I acknowledge receipt of your Notification of issuance of the Certificate dated Nov.5th. Unfortunately, we have not been paid yet, and all attempts on our part to contact Bill Durr have been snubbed. Could you help out on this one please?

Yours

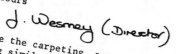 J. Wesmey (Director)

P.S. I believe the carpeting supplier, Walter Wall is having similar problems.

P.P.S. I hear that Mr Square is converting a windmill for his own use. I'm sending over a few hundred quarries which should come in handy.

Reg.Office : 2, The Barricades, Cringing, Wilts.

WILLIAM DURR ESQ
Building Contractor

2, The Bitter End
Cringing,
Wilts.

23.11.94

Dear Mr Fair,

re: Development at Letsby Avenue.

In accordance with the Contract provisions, we are requesting a three week extension to the contract time to allow for a period of inclement weather, incorrect instructions from your good selves and a labour problems caused by manpower shortages and a wildcat strike.

Would you please alter the completion date accordingly?

Yours sincerely,

W. Durr.

W.Durr, LCIOB.

DESK DIARY

NOV 25

re: Wesmey-Shovelgon
NSC/W is in operation here, so we can
demand proof of payment from Durr- No proof,
and employer pays direct (35.13.5). Might also
mention supplier, but nothing we can do here.
Acknowledge Wesmey's letter, and tell him
what we are doing.

NOV 26

NO

Fair and Square

CHARTERED ARCHITECTS

B°.FAIR.dip.arch.RIBA.
T.SQUARE.B.Arch.RIBA.AFAS.

4, The Hellovet
Cringing,
Wilts.

26.11.94

ᵇᶠ/vn

re: Development at Letsby Avenue, Cringing.

Dear Mr Durr,

We acknowledge receipt of your letter dated 23rd November, the
contents of which we note. We would draw your attention to
Clause 25.2.1.1. of the Standard Form, and therefore require
further information concerning the material circumstances of
the delays you mention, and identification where appropriate
of the Relevant Event.

We also look forward to receiving as soon as possible
particulars of the anticipated effects of each Relevant Ev
and your estimate of the expected delay in the completion
the work.

We are confident that you will use your best efforts to
minimise the effects of any delays, and assure you of ou
action as soon as we have heard from you.

Yours sincerely,

Fair & Square

Fair and Square.

William Durr Esq,
2, The Bitter End,
Cringing,
Wilts.

Fair and Square

CHARTERED ARCHITECTS

B.FAIR.dip.arch.RIBA.
T.SQUARE.B.Arch.RIBA.AFAS.

BF/vn

4,The Hellovet,
Cringing,
Wilts.

16.11.94

Dear Mr Chargeer,

I received your telephone message
yesterday regarding a new bay window and an extra wing
to your new development in Letsby Avenue. Before
proceeding, we will have to check:
A) If the extra work will require
further Local Authority permissions.
B) Whether or not the additions you want
(particularly the new wing) constitute a 'material'
change to the contract, in which case a Variation will be
insufficient, and a new contract will have to be drawn up.

When we have established these points, we will be able
to advise you as to the added cost of the work, and the
extra time beyond the present Completion Date that will
be necessary for design and construction

MEMO

To

From : Tom

ate : Bill

: 23rd Nov.

ncerning :Wesmey's free quarries
Have these arrived yet? A nice
thought, but you'd better send
them back (remember the f
with profuse tha

SECTION SEVEN

COMPLETION

Contents

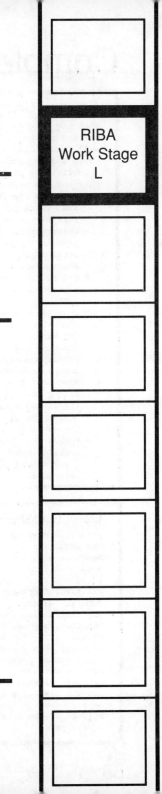

RIBA
Work Stage
L

Completion

Practical Completion (Clause 17)

When the work is completed except for very minor matters and there are no defects, the architect will inspect the work. If, in his opinion, all tests and inspections prove to be satisfactory, a Certificate of Practical Completion is issued. This has the effect of:

- Allowing the release of half the retention sum, which the employer must pay within 14 days of the receipt by the employer of the next interim certificate (provisions may be made in the contract for the release of retained sums owing to sub-contractors who finish early).
- Ending the responsibility of the employer or contractor to insure the property under the contract.
- Enabling the employer to take possession, upon which the employer should adjust his insurance cover accordingly.
- Starting the Defects Liability Period which, if not specified in the Appendix, will be 6 months from the date of the Certificate of Practical Completion.
- Ending the contractor's liability for liquidated damages.
- Ending the contractor's liability for damage caused by frost occurring thereafter.
- Ending the issue of regular interim certificates.
- Allowing any reference to arbitration to be opened.

Defects Liability Period

Within 14 days of the expiration of this period, the architect must provide the contractor with a Schedule of Defects specifying any materials or workmanship not in accordance with the contract, including frost damage occurring prior to Practical Completion. The contractor must make good the defects within a reasonable time. At any time during the Defects Liability Period, the architect may require the making good of defects if he considers it necessary. When the work has been corrected to make it accord with the contract provisions, the architect will issue a Certificate of Making Good Defects. Upon issuance of this (or the expiration of the Defects Liability Period, whichever is the later), the architect authorises release of the balance of the retained sum in the next interim certificate.

Final Certificate (Clause 30)

This is issued before the end of 2 months from the latest of the following:

- The end of the Defects Liability Period
- Issuance of the Making Good of Defects Certificate
- The sending of ascertainment and statement of final sum to the contractor

At this point or possibly earlier, a continuing liability period begins for the architect and the contractor as established by the Limitation Acts 1939 and 1980. this is normally 6 years, but extends to 12 if the contract is made as a deed. In tort, the position is more complex (see page 11).

Partial Possession (Clause 18)

The employer, with the contractor's consent (not to be unreasonably withheld) may take over a completed part of the building while the rest of the building work continues. the architect must issue a Written Statement identifying the part and the relevant date. Procedures are similar to Practical Completion, except that the value of the relevant part only is used for calculations, the amounts of retention and liquidated damages are proportionally reduced, and the contractor or the employer as appropriate reduces the amount of insurance accordingly.

Handover Meetings

It may be convenient to hold a handover meeting at the end of the project, when inspections may be made and the building, site, owner's manual, keys, as-built drawings etc. passed into the employer's possession.

Extra Services

Services offered by the architect after completion of the project might include:

- An evaluation of the structure in occupation.
- A maintenance contract of ongoing inspection at regular intervals.

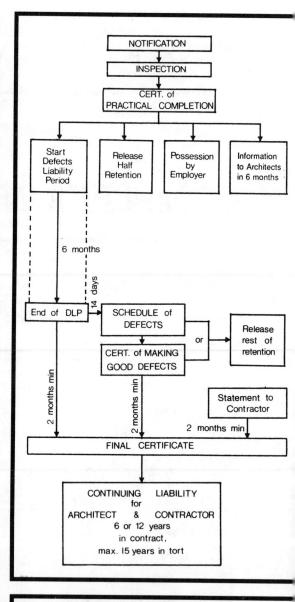

R
E
F
ARCHITECT'S JOB BOOK. pp. 129-145.
THE ARCHITECT'S GUIDE TO RUNNING
A JOB. pp. 140-151.
THE ARCHITECT IN PRACTICE. pp. 233-244.

Certificate of

Practical Completion

Issued by: FAIR AND SQUARE
address: 4, THE HELLOVET, CRINGING, WILTS

Employer: HUSSEIN CHARGEER
address: 1, LETSBY AVENUE, CRINGING, WILTS

Job reference: 8072

Certificate no: 1

Contractor: WILLIAM DURR LTD
address: 2, THE BITTER END, CRINGING, WILTS

Issue date: 13 January 1994

Works: NEW DETACHED HOUSE
situated at: 1, LETSBY AVENUE, CRINGING, WILTS

Contract dated: 29 January 1993

Under the terms of the above-mentioned Contract,

I/we hereby certify that Practical Completion of

*Delete as
appropriate

*1. the Works

*2. Section No xxxxxxxxxx of the Works

was achieved on

7 January   19 94

To be signed by or for
the issuer named
above

Signed _Fair & Square_

Distribution	Original to:	Duplicate to:	Copies to:	
	☐ Employer	☐ Contractor	☐ Quantity Surveyor	☐ Clerk of Works
			☐ Consultants	☐ File

Certificate of
Completion of

**Making Good
Defects**

Issued by: FAIR AND SQUARE
address: 4, THE HELLOVET, CRINGING, WILTS

Employer: HUSSEIN CHARGEER
address: 1, LETSBY AVENUE, CRINGING, WILTS

Job reference: 8072

Certificate no: 1

Contractor: WILLIAM DURR LTD
address: 2, THE BITTER END, CRINGING, WILTS

Issue date: 26 July 1994

Works: NEW DETACHED HOUSE
situated at: 1, LETSBY AVENUE, CRINGING, WILTS

Contract dated: 29 January 1993

Under the terms of the above-mentioned Contract,

I/we hereby certify that the defects, shrinkages and other faults specified
in the schedule of defects delivered to the Contractor as an instruction have
in my/our opinion been made good.

This Certificate refers to:

*Delete as
appropriate

*1. the Works referred to in the
Certificate of Practical Completion

No. 1   dated 13 January 1994

*2. Section No. xxxxxxxxx of the Works referred to in the
Certificate of Practical Completion

No. xxxxxxxxxx dated xx

*3. the part of the Works identified in the
Statement/Certificate of Partial Possession by the Employer

No. xxxxxxxxxx dated xx

To be signed by or for
the issuer named
above

Signed _Fair & Square_

Distribution	Original to:	Duplicate to:	Copies to:	
	☐1 Employer	☐1 Contractor	☐1 Quantity Surveyor	☐1 Clerk of Works
			☐1 Consultants	☐1 File

F807 for JCT 80 / IFC 84 / MW 80

© RIBA Publications Ltd 1990

Issued by: FAIR AND SQUARE
address: 4, THE HELLOVET, CRINGING, WILTS

**Final
Certificate**

Employer: HUSSEIN CHARGEER
address: 1, LETSBY AVENUE, CRINGING, WILTS

Serial no: **A 000228**

Job reference: 8072

Contractor: WILLIAM DURR LTD
address: 2, THE BITTER END, CRINGING, WILTS

Issue date: 9 August 1994

Contract sum: £156,000

Works: NEW DETACHED HOUSE
situated at: 1, LETSBY AVENUE, CRINGING, WILTS

Contract dated: 29 January 1993

Original to Employer

This Final Certificate is issued under the terms of the above-mentioned Contract.

The Contract Sum adjusted as necessary is . . . .   £ 167,000.00

The total amount previously certified for payment to the Contractor is . . . .   £ 159,000.00

The difference between the above-stated amounts is . . . .   £   8,000.00

I/We hereby certify the sum of (in words)
 Eight thousand pounds only

as a **balance due**:

*Delete as
appropriate

*to the Contractor from the Employer.

*~~to the Employer from the Contractor~~

All amounts are exclusive of VAT

To be signed by or for
the issuer named
above

Signed   *Fair & Square*

The terms of the Contract provide that, subject to any amounts properly deductible by the Employer, the said balance shall be a debt payable from the one to the other as from the

[1] Delete as
appropriate. See cover
notes for provision in
particular contract.

[1] x ~~14th / 21st~~ / 28th day after the date of this Certificate.

[2] Relevant only if
clause 1A of JCT 80
VAT Agreement,
clause A1-1 of IFC 84
Supplemental
Conditions or clause
B1-1 of MW 80
Supplementary
Memorandum applies.
Delete if not
applicable.

[2] ~~The Contractor has given notice that the rate of VAT chargeable on the supply of goods and services to which the Contract relates is~~   %

[2] _____ % of the amount certified above is . . . .   £

[2] ~~Total of balance due and VAT amount (for information)~~ . . . . £

This is not a Tax Invoice

F852   for JCT 80 / IFC 84 / MW 80

© RIBA Publications Ltd 1990

FINAL STATEMENT OF ACCOUNT

Employer ..... HUSSEIN CHARGEER ....

Project ..... 1 LETSBY AVENUE ....

Quantity Surveyor
ASA RULE
....

Architect
FAIR AND SQUARE
....

Contractor ..... WILLIAM DURR LTD ....

Ref ..... 8072 ....   Date ..... 9 AUGUST 1988

Amount of Contract							156,000	00
LESS Contingencies							5,000	00
							151,000	00
LESS Adjustment of P.C. and Provisional Sums							500	00
							150,500	00
ADD Adjustment of Measured Work							12,250	00
							162,750	00
ADD Contractor's claims for Loss and Expense under Clause 26							4,250	00
				AMOUNT OF FINAL ACCOUNT			167,000	00

Contractor's Signature

W. Durr ....

Date .... 9.8.94.

LOCKE, STOCKE and BARRELL.

A.Locke.LLB(Lond).
J.Stocke.MA(Oxon).
B.Barrell.BA(Rangoon).

SOLICITORS

Our Ref: BB/as
Your Ref:

1, Fore Hall,
Cringing,
Wilts.

9.12.94

Dear Sirs,

      re: House at Rock Bottom, Cringing.

We are acting for Mr Justice Ongatt-Wylitte in respect of his above
property of which you were the architects in charge nine years ago.
Last year, our client discovered signs of serious subsidence in the
foundations of his house. This condition has now worsened, and
considerable work will be required to restore the property to its
full value.

We are at present seeking estimates in order to assess the loss which
our client has suffered as a result of your negligence. When these
estimates are to hand, it is our proposal to appoint an arbitrator
in accordance with the terms of the agreement between yourselves and
our client should you be unwilling to admit your full responsibility
in this matter.

We look forward to receiving your comments.

               Yours sincerely,

               Locke Stocke & Barrell

               Locke, Stocke and Barrell.

TELEPHONE MESSAGE

Time 9.15 a.m.   Date 14 Dec.

From 1.Sawyer   To F & S.

Concerning Letsby Ave. job. Says
our old c. of w. rang. Says
he passed Chargeer's place
yesterday & thought that
equipment & possibly some
materials were being removed
- he thought we should know - do
you know anything about this
Bill?

Taken By Tom S.

8, The Lot,
CRINGING,
WILTS.

15th Dec.

Dear Mr Fair,
        I am writing to you about the house
you designed for me last year. I am very happy
with it, although another little problem has
cropped up.

You remember the puddle that collected on the flat
roof after that rain a couple of months ago? And
you said it was nothing to worry about? Well,
the guttering around that part of the roof
doesn't seem to be discharging properly, and
I would be grateful if you would come over
and have a look at it.

               With kind regards,

               A. Badger.

               A. Badger.

MEMO

To   : Tom
From   : Roy Tring
Date   : December 14.
Concerning : Chargeers. job.

1 Saw DURR this morning - He's
insisting that the bricks he ordered
the job are unobtainable due to
labour strikes & wants to
the contract as a...

DESK DIARY

DEC 14

re: Letsby Ave/removal of equipment :-
I'll check this out today in person - Durr may
only be clearing up.
Materials paid for mustn't be removed, &
those on site not paid for not to be removed
without our permission.
I'll remind Durr of this if the report seems to
be accurate & inform Chargeer & see what he
wants to do. Better bone up on Determination -
Just in case
B.F.

DEC 15

re: 'unobtainable(?)' bricks.
Lets explore other alternatives (other suppliers
variation of the works etc) before we talk about
determination - it's early days yet.
In any case, Durr's contract with the supplier
seems to have been broken & he should
pursue his rights here.

DEC 16

Send to
L.S & Barrell.

Fair and Square

CHARTERED ARCHITECTS

B.FAIR.dip.arch.RIBA.
T.SQUARE.B.Arch.RIBA.AFAS.

4, The Hellov
Cringing,
Wilts.

BF/vn

22.12.94

Dear Mr Badger,
Thank you for your letter of the 15th December.
We are sorry to hear you still feel you have a problem with your
roof. As you know, Mr Fair visited your house on a number of
occasions since it was completed, and found nothing really to
worry about - perhaps a simple maintenance job is all that is
required.

We will of course be happy to visit you again if you wish,
and enclose a copy of the Standard Form of Agreement for
the Appointment of an Architect, together with details of
fees and expenses
We look forward to hearing from you.

Yours sincerely,

Fair & Square.

Fair and Square.

Square

Architects

4, The Hellovet,
Cringing,
Wilts.

RE : House at Rock Bottom, Cringing.

We acknowledge receipt of your communication
dated 9.12.94 which is receiving our attention.

Bill - remember the Rock Bottom House? Trouble.
I've acknowledged L.S.B's letter & checked the files.
Our ex-partner Arthur Mild was responsible for the job
before he retired. We'd better check the partnership
agreement and inform Arthur, our insurers and
solicitors in view of the Latent Damage
Act 1986.

Tom.

SECTION EIGHT

ARBITRATION

Contents	Pages	Contents	Page

Determination

For a variety of reasons, not all contracts are fully performed. A contract can be discharged in a number of ways (see page 54), but the 1980 Standard Form makes special provision for the determination of the contractor's employment under the building contract. Of course, the common law rights of both the employer and the contractor may also be invoked.

By the Employer (Clause 27)

The employer may end the contractor's employment:
- If the contractor entirely or substantially suspends the progress of the works.
- If the contractor fails to regularly and diligently proceed with the works.
- If the contractor persistently fails to comply with the architect's written notices requiring defective work to be removed.
- If the contractor sub-lets or assigns a part of the work without permission as detailed in Clause 19.

Procedure

The architect specifies the particular default to the contractor by registered post, recorded or actual delivery. Upon receipt of this notice, if the contractor continues the default for 14 days, the employer may determine the contractor's employment within the following 10 days or on repetition thereafter. Notice of determination must be given by registered post, recorded or actual delivery. If a provisional liquidator or trustee in bankruptcy is appointed or a winding up order is made, the contractor's employment is automatically determined, but it may be reinstated if the parties agree. In all other cases of insolvency, the employer may determine the contractor's employment unless the parties agree to proceed with or novate the contract and until such time the employer need make no further payment and the contractor need do no further work. The employer does not have the right to set-off in respect of payment under any interim arrangement. The employer may take reasonable steps to protect the site, the works and any materials on site. The employer may also determine if the contractor is guilty of any corrupt act.

After determination the employer can:
- Pay others to finish the work, using the contractor's equipment etc. on site.
- By written instruction of the architect, order the contractor to remove the equipment and, if not so removed within a reasonable time, sell it, holding all the proceeds (save for expenses incurred) to the contractor's credit.
- Demand from the contractor payment in respect of direct loss or damage caused by the determination.
- Take over the benefits of agreements with sub-contractors and suppliers, and pay them directly.

- Make no further payments to the contractor until after completion and making good of defects in the works and the final cost to the employer has been established.
- Opt, within 6 months of the determination, not to continue with the works and to prepare an account showing the balance owing between the parties after all the employer's expenses have been taken into account.

By the Contractor (Clause 28)

The contractor may end his employment:
- If the employer has not paid the sums due to him within 14 days of the issuance of a certificate.
- If the employer obstructs or interferes with the issuance of a certificate.
- If substantially the whole works are suspended for a period named in the Appendix due to loss or damage to the works caused by:
  - Certain architect's instructions.
  - Late provision of information requested by the contractor in writing at a time not unreasonably distant of close to the date required.
  - Delay by the employer in work not included in the contract, or supplies undelivered.
  - If the employer fails to give access.

and the employer has not remedied the default within 14 days of receipt of notice by registered post, recorded or actual delivery. The contractor may determine without prior notice if the employer becomes insolvent.

Procedure

The contractor should inform the employer of the determination by registered post, recorded or actual delivery. He may then:
- Remove his equipment, temporary buildings etc.(taking precautions for safety).
- Be paid the total retention within 28 days of the date of determination.
- Claim the total value of work executed at the date of determination.
- Claim direct loss or damage caused by the determination (and also loss suffered by nominated sub-contractors).
- Claim costs of removal.
- Claim costs of materials and goods paid for, and properly ordered in connection with the work (upon payment, they become the employer's property).

The contractor is responsible for preparing this account and the employer must pay the amount properly due within 28 days of submission with no deduction of retention.

By either Party (Clause 28A)

Either party may determine the contractor's employment if substantially the whole of the uncompleted works are suspended for a continuous period named in the Appendix due to:
- Force majeure
- A Specified Peril
- Civil commotion
- Architect's instructions regarding discrepancies, variations or postponement due to the negligence of a local authority or statutory undertaker
- Hostilities
- Terrorist activity

and on the expiry of the suspension period the employer or the contractor gives notice by registered post, recorded or actual delivery that the employment will determine within 7 days after receipt of such notice.

Procedure

The consequences are broadly the same as if the contractor determines under clause 28 except that he may not claim loss or damage to himself or a nominated sub-contractor caused by the determination unless due to Specified Perils. The employer must prepare the account on receipt of documentation from the contractor within 2 months of the date of determination and discharge the amount within 28 days of submission to the contractor without deduction of retention.

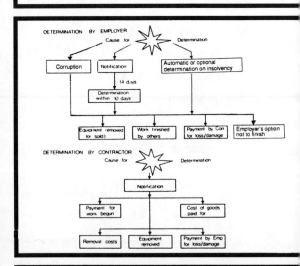

REF   LAW MADE SIMPLE. pp. 167-176.

The Courts/Arbitration

If all other remedies and mechanisms have failed to provide a satisfactory conclusion to a contractual disagreement, a third party may be called upon to settle the matter.

The third party may be a civil judge or registrar in the case of normal court actions (see page 7). Alternatively, a dispute may be settled by ARBITRATION.

Whereas the courts are part of the English Legal System and therefore subject to all its procedural and administrative elements, problems submitted to arbitration enjoy a private and informal hearing in the presence of (usually) whoever they choose. The arbitrator (or arbitrators) is often someone with a specific knowledge and experience in the field in which the dispute has arisen, and in building, is often an architect or surveyor who belongs to the Chartered Institute of Arbitrators.

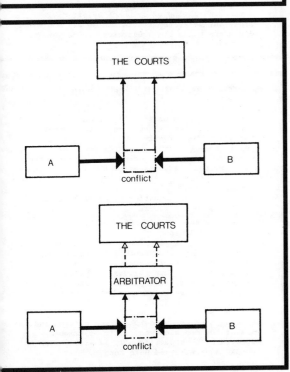

Advantages

- PRIVACY
- CONVENIENCE
- SPEED
- EXPENSE
- SIMPLICITY
- EXPERTISE

a PRIVACY
Trade secrets and reputations may be shielded from the public in a private arbitration. This would not be possible in the courts, where hearings are public.

b CONVENIENCE
The hearing can be held anywhere to suit the parties. (for example, on the site of the dispute).

c SPEED
Disputes can be handled quickly, without the inconvenience of having to fit into the courts' timetable. In projects where time is of the essence, this may be an important factor.

d EXPENSE
Money might be saved both in the potentially lower cost of the hearing, and in the speedy resolution of the problem.

e SIMPLICITY
Courtroom procedures may be dispensed with, according to the nature of the dispute. It is within the arbitrator's discretion to decide upon the level of informality to employ.

f EXPERTISE
Difficult construction-oriented problems may be better understood by an experienced arbitrator with knowledge in this field rather than a professional judge.

Disadvantages

- COST
- LACK OF LEGAL EXPERTISE
- PRECEDENT

a COST
In some cases, an escalation of hired help (solicitors, barristers, expert witnesses etc.) can lead to high costs. The arbitrator and place of hearing must also be paid for, which in the courts system is free.

b LACK OF LEGAL EXPERTISE
The arbitrator, although knowledgeable in the field of the dispute, might lack a detailed understanding of the law.

c PRECEDENT
Although the arbitrator is bound to follow the precedents of case law, the advantage of privacy makes it inevitable that there is no collection of precedents available from completed arbitrations. This may make it difficult for a prospective party to an arbitration to assess the likelihood of success.

When to Arbitrate

A matter may be referred to arbitration by:
- AGREEMENT BEFORE THE DISPUTE (possibly in the contract)
- AGREEMENT AFTER THE DISPUTE
- OPERATION OF LAW (by statute or court order).

Most construction contracts contain a provision allowing for arbitration (for example, Standard Form Article 5). Although no party can be denied access to the courts, ignoring an arbitration clause breaches the contract so that the courts, upon application, will often stay court proceedings, leaving arbitration as the sole remedy.

Arbitration Procedure 1

All arbitration agreements, as long as they are formed in writing, are governed by the Arbitration Acts 1950 to 1979, which provide that:
- The arbitrator's authority is irrevocable (unless revoked by the High Court).
- The arbitrator's award is final and binding (except for certain clearly defined situations).
- The award, if registered in the courts, will be enforceable.

This means that, although separate from the court structure, certain connections between the High Court and arbitration exist:

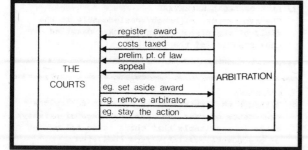

Selection

The arbitrator (or arbitrators) may be chosen:

- By agreement prior to the dispute
- By agreement after the dispute
- By application to a third party (The Chartered Institute of Arbitrators, perhaps, or in the case of the Standard Form, usually the President or Vice-President of the Royal Institute of British Architects).

Upon being asked to act in an arbitration, an arbitrator must assess the suitability of an arbitration to the particular dispute, and his own suitability to act. Factors preventing him from accepting the commission would include personal knowledge of one of the parties, or an interest or bias in the matters affected.

If the arbitrator decides to act, both parties are notified. It is advisable at this stage to secure a deposit from both parties.

Directors

Prior to the actual hearing, the arbitrator will direct certain preliminary matters to be undertaken by both parties so that the precise points of the dispute are clear. Preliminary correspondence and meetings (if any) should provide for:

- Points of Claim by the claimant.
- Points of Defence by the respondent, together with a Counterclaim, if any.
- Defence to the Counterclaim by the claimant, if appropriate.

These points should contain facts about the dispute only, and no evidence. If either side is unclear as to the other's claim or defence, they may apply for Further and Better Particulars.

Further matters to be considered include:

- The discovery of all documents concerned with the dispute.
- The number of experts (solicitors barristers, expert witnesses etc.) required or limited to each side.
- Figures involved to be agreed if possible.
- Shorthand provisions. Usually, the arbitrator takes his own notes, but with the agreement of parties, assistance may be provided.
- The liberty of either party to apply (for amendments etc.).
- Whether to include the right to appeal.

The Hearing

The date, time and location of the hearing will be established in correspondence or at preliminary meetings. Should a party refuse to attend or be deliberately obstructive, the arbitrator, with an order from the High Court, may commence with the proceedings EX PARTE (that is, in his absence), provided that the absentee has been informed of his right to attend.

The procedure of the hearing is likely to follow that of a court of law, abiding by the rules of evidence, although the arbitrator has wide powers to conduct the hearing depending upon the circumstances and the wishes of the parties.

JCT Arbitration Rules 1988

JCT forms of contract now provide for arbitrations to be carried out under the JCT Arbitration Rules 1988. They include three procedures for the conduct of the arbitration:

- Rule 5: Procedures without a hearing
- Rule 6: Full procedure with a hearing
- Rule 7: Short procedure with a hearing

Rule 5 is to be used unless the parties jointly agree either of rules 6 or 7 or unless the arbitrator, having heard representations, directs that rule 6 is to be used.

The rules contain strict time scales for the steps to be taken by the parties and sanctions for failure to meet those times. The arbitrator is also to act within specified periods.

In addition to other powers conferred by law, the arbitrator is given power to:
- take legal or technical advice
- give directions for protecting, storing or disposing of property which is the subject of the dispute
- order a party to give security for costs
- proceed in the absence of a party after reasonable notice
- direct that costs be taxed by the arbitrator
- direct the giving of evidence by affidavit
- order any party to produce and supply copies of documents which the arbitrator decides are relevant

Alternative Dispute Resolution

This is an alternative to arbitration or litigation. It is essentially mediation or concilliation. It is not binding on the parties, therefore to be effective, the parties must honestly wish to settle their differences. If they are not successful, they are free to pursue their legal remedies. Advantages of ADR are said to be:
- Saving of time
- Saving of money
- Promotes the continuation of cordial trading relations in the future

ADR can take many forms, but usually derives from one of the following:
- <u>Concilliation or mediation</u>: The mediator consults with both parties separately to seek common ground and areas of compromise. The mediator may be asked for his conclusions and proposals.
- <u>Mini-trial</u>: Each side presents a short case to a tribunal consisting of a mediator and a senior person from each side who then retire to settle the matter.

ADR depends on the goodwill of the parties and the skill of the mediator who should be someone respected by both parties. It is widely used in the USA, Australia and Hong Kong.

Costs and the Award

Throughout the hearing, the arbitrator must apply the ordinary law. He is bound to follow past decisions of the courts in deciding the case.

When the hearing closes, the arbitrator must, within a reasonable time, make an award. No reasons need be given for the final decision or any other details, unless one of the parties, before the award, requests reasons. In this case, the High Court can order reasons to be given. The award may simply state who won and who is to bear the costs of the arbitration, including the arbitrator's fees. It is now becoming normal for both parties to require the arbitrator to give reasons. Notification that the award is complete is then given to both parties. Either may pick up the award, but must pay the arbitrator's fee before doing so. If the collecting party has won the dispute, he will usually be reimbursed for the fee by the loser, as costs generally follow the event.

The Expert Witness

It is possible that an architect may be called to an arbitration to give his expert opinion regarding matters concerning a building dispute. Whereas the ordinary witness gives evidence of the facts as observed, the expert witness gives an opinion based upon those facts. He is not usually connected with the case before the dispute, and is called by one of the parties because his evidence supports their particular case.

It is usual for each party to provide their own expert witness (or witnesses), and to pay the appropriate fees involved in their employment. Although opinions given by expert witnesses on opposing sides of a dispute are likely to differ, they must be made in good faith and be sincerely held. It is the expert's duty to assist the arbitrator to arrive at the truth.

Appeals & Points of Law

The High Court no longer has jurisdiction to set aside or remit an award on the grounds of errors of fact or law on the face of the award. Instead, it is possible to bring an appeal on a question of law arising out of an award either with the consent of all parties to the reference or, in certain circumstances, with leave of the court. However, both parties can, in writing, agree to exclude the right to appeal, thus making the award truly final and binding, provided that such an agreement is made **after** the arbitration has commenced.

In limited circumstances, application may be made to the court to determine a PRELIMINARY POINT OF LAW if either the arbitrator or all parties to the reference agree. The court must be satisfied that substantial cost savings will be made, and that the question of law is one in respect of which an appeal might later be brought.

The Architect as Arbitrator

Professional qualification and experience in the field of architecture suggests an expertise in the construction field which may provide a foundation for arbitration work. The Chartered Institute of Arbitrators runs a number of courses and examinations for prospective members who wish to apply for Associateship or Fellowship.

Further information may be obtained from:

THE CHARTERED INSTITUTE OF ARBITRATORS
24 Angel Gate
City Road
London EC1V 2RS

R
E
F

RIBA 'THE ARCHITECT AS ARBITRATOR'.
LAW MADE SIMPLE. pp. 72-74.
PRACTICE MANAGEMENT HANDBOOK.
PP. 62-64.
ARCHITECT'S LEGAL HANDBOOK. pp. 156-168.

IN THE MATTER OF THE ARBITRATION ACTS 1950 - 1979
AND IN THE MATTER OF AN ARBITRATION
BETWEEN :

_____ (claimant)

and

_____ (respondent)

Whereas by an agreement made in writing on the .... day of .... 19...
between the claimant of the one part and the respondent of the other
part, it was agreed that in the event of a dispute arising from
matters set out in the said agreement, either party could make
application to the President or a Vice-President for the time being
of the Royal Institute of British Architects to appoint a single
arbitrator.

And whereas a dispute having arisen between the parties, the President
for the time being of the Royal Institute of British Architects
did, on the ...day of ... 19... appoint me ....
to be sole arbitrator.

Now I, the said ...., having accepted the said appointment, and having heard and considered the allegations, witnesses
and evidence of both parties (and addresses made to me on their
behalf), and having inspected the premises at _____
on the .... day of .... 19..., do hereby make and publish this my
award.

That : 1. The sum of £... to be paid by the (Respondent) to the
(Claimant) in full and final settlement in respect of all matters
pleaded before me within 30 days of this award being taken up.

That : 2. The (Respondent) shall pay the costs of the (Claimant)
on a party and party basis, such costs to be taxed if not agreed.

That : 3. The (Respondent) shall pay and bear the costs of my
award, which I tax and settle in the sum of £... including VAT,
or if such costs have already been paid by the (Claimant) repay
such costs to the (Claimant).

Made and published by me the said ...., this
.... day of .... 19...

_____
                         Arbitrator.

Signed in the presence of

_____
Witness
(including address and occupation).

ARCHITECTS' BENEVOLENT SOCIETY
66 Portland Place
London W1N 4AD

CONSTRUCTION INDUSTRY INFORMATION GROUP
26 Store Street
London WC1E 7BT

ARCHITECTS' REGISTRATION COUNCIL OF THE
UNITED KINGDOM
73, Hallam Street
London W1N 6EE

INSTITUTE OF ARCHITECTS AND SURVEYORS
15 St Mary Street
Chippenham
Wilts SN15 3JN

BARBOUR INDEX LTD
New Lodge,
Drift Road,
Windsor,
Berks SL4 4RQ

GOVERNMENT BOOKSHOPS
Her Majesty's Stationery Office
49 High Holborn
London WC1V 6HB

INCORPORATED ASSOCIATION OF ARCHITECTS
AND SURVEYORS
Jubilee House
Billing Brook Road
Weston Favell
Northampton NN3 4NW

NATIONAL BUILDING SPECIFICATION LTD
Mansion House Chambers
The Close
Newcastle-upon-Tyne NE1 3RE

BUILDING RESEARCH ESTABLISHMENT
Garston
Watford WD2 7JR

CONSTRUCTION INDUSTRY COMPUTING ASSOCIATION
Guildhall Place
Cambridge CB2 3QQ

CHARTERED INSTITUTE OF ARBITRATORS
24 Angel Gate
City Road
London EC1V 2RS

ROYAL INSTITUTE OF BRITISH ARCHITECTS
66 Portland Place
London W1N 4AD

Useful Addresses 2

RIBA SERVICES LTD (LEGAL AND VAT ADVICE)
AND
RIBA PUBLICATIONS LTD
Finsbury Mission
Moreland Street
London EC1V 8VB

ROYAL INSTITUTION OF CHARTERED SURVEYORS
12 Great George Street
Parliament Square
London SW1P 3AD

BRITISH INSTITUTE OF ARCHITECTURAL TECHNICIANS
397 City Road
London EC1V 1NE

PLANNING
To obtain planning appeal forms and information
regarding procedure, write to:

IN ENGLAND
The Planning Inspectorate
Department of the Environment and Transport
Tollgate House
Houlton Street
Bristol BS2 9DJ

IN WALES
Welsh Office
Planning Division
Cathays Park
Cardiff CF1 3NQ

If it is believed that the appeal procedure
is not satisfactorily adhered to, details
should be sent to:

Secretary of the Council on Tribunals
22 Kingsway
London WC2B 6LE

Select Bibliography

These books have been used as reference sources throughout the text.

COX, Stanley; MALES, Roderick;
BEAVEN, Leonard and DRY, David.
'ARCHITECT'S JOB BOOK'. 5th Edition 1991.
RIBA PUBLICATIONS LTD, LONDON.

DAVIS, Lawrence
'GUIDE TO THE BUILDING REGULATIONS 1991,
1992 BUTTERWORTH-HEINEMANN, OXFORD.

GREEN, Ronald
'THE ARCHITECT'S GUIDE TO RUNNING A JOB'.
4th Revised Edition 1986.
BUTTERWORTH-HEINEMANN, OXFORD.

'HANDBOOK OF ARCHITECTURAL PRACTICE MANAGEMENT'.
5th Edition, 1991. RIBA PUBLICATIONS LTD,
LONDON.

BARKER, David and PADFIELD, Colin
'LAW MADE SIMPLE'. 8th Edition, Revised 1993.
BUTTERWORTH-HEINEMANN, OXFORD.

SPEAIGHT, Anthony and STONE, Gregory (Editors).
'ARCHITECT'S LEGAL HANDBOOK'. 5th Edition,
1990. BUTTERWORTH-HEINEMANN, OXFORD.

CHAPPELL, David and WILLIS, Christopher.
'THE ARCHITECT IN PRACTICE'.
7th Edition 1992
BLACKWELL SCIENTIFIC PUBLICATIONS, OXFORD.

Further Reading

These books are recommended for reference where a more extensive coverage of a subject area is required.

CHAPPELL, David.
'STANDARD LETTERS IN ARCHITECTURAL PRACTICE',
2ND EDITION 1993.
BLACKWELL SCIENTIFIC PUBLICATIONS, OXFORD.

CECIL, Ray.
'PROFESSIONAL LIABILITY'. 3rd Edition, 1991.
LEGAL STUDIES AND SERVICES (PUBLISHING).

CHAPPELL, David.
'CONTRACTUAL CORRESPONDENCE FOR ARCHITECTS',
2nd Edition 1989.
LEGAL STUDIES AND SERVICES (PUBLISHING).

'PLANNING APPLICATIONS: THE RMJM GUIDE'
2nd Edition, 1991.
BLACKWELL SCIENTIFIC PUBLICATIONS LTD. OXFORD,

CRESSWELL, H.B.
'THE HONEYWOOD FILE & THE HONEYWOOD
SETTLEMENT' 1929-1930 Reprint 1983.
BUTTERWORTH-HEINEMANN, OXFORD

Bibliography 2

HEAP, Desmond.
'AN OUTLINE OF PLANNING LAW'.
9th Revised Edition, 1987. SWEET & MAXWELL,
LONDON

KEATING, Don and MAY, Anthony.
'BUILDING CONTRACTS'.
5th Revised Edition, 1991.
SWEET & MAXWELL,
LONDON.

POWELL-SMITH, V. and SIMS, J.
'CONSTRUCTIONS-A PRACTICAL GUIDE', 1989.
LEGAL STUDIES AND SERVICES (PUBLISHING),
LONDON.

RIBA PUBLICATIONS:
Useful RIBA Publications include:

'Group Practice and Consortia'.

'Starting Up in Practice' 1992.

'Guide to Employment Practice' 1987.

'The Architect as Arbitrator' 1987.

'Code of Professional Conduct' 1991.

'SFA' 1992.

'JCT Gude to the 1980 Editions of the Standard
Forms'.

'The 1990-91 Planning Acts - A Plain English
Guide With Case Law References'. 1992.

MADGE, Peter.
'Responsibilities for Insurance under the JCT
Standard Form of Contract' 1989.
Open Learning Package.

MALES, Roderick.
'Principles and Procedures Associated
with Sub-contractors and Suppliers,
1989. Open Learning Package.

NJCC PUBLICATIONS:

'Code of Procedure for Single Stage Selective
Tendering' 1989.

'Code of Procedure for Two Stage Selective
Tendering' 1983.

PITT, Peter.
'GUIDE TO BUILDING CONTROL IN INNER LONDON'.
1987.
BUTTERWORTH-HEINEMANN,
OXFORD.

PITT, Peter.
'GUIDE TO BUILDING CONTROL BY LOCAL ACTS 1987'.
1987.
BUTTERWORTH-HEINEMANN,
OXFORD.

UFF, John.
'CONSTRUCTION LAW'.
5th Edition, 1991. SWEET & MAXWELL, LONDON.

WALLACE, Duncan.
'HUDSON'S BUILDING AND ENGINEERING CONTRACTS'.
10th Edition, 1970, 1st Supplement 1981.
SWEET & MAXWELL, LONDON.

POWELL-SMITH, V and BILLINGTON, M. '
THE BUILDING REGULATIONS EXPLAINED AND
ILLUSTRATED'.
9th Revised Edition, 1992.
BLACKWELL SCIENTIFIC PUBLICATIONS, OXFORD.

POWELL-SMITH, V and CHAPPELL, D.
'BUILDING CONTRACT DICTIONARY'. 2nd Edition,
1990.
LEGAL STUDIES AND SERVICES, LONDON.

Cases

Statutes

Table of Statutes

Glossary

Glossary of Common Legal Terms

Ab initio	from the beginning
Bona fide	in good faith
Caveat emptor	let the buyer beware
Ejusdem generis	of the same type
Estoppel	a rule of evidence which prevents a person from denying or asserting a fact owing to a previous act.
Ex parte	upon the application of
Ignorantia juris non excusat	ignorance of the law is no excuse
In personam	against a person i.e. not against everyone
In rem	against a thing i.e. applicable to everyone
Inter se	amongst themselves
Obiter dicta	things said by the way
Per se	by itself
Prima facie	on first view
Quantum meruit	as much as he deserves
Ratio decidendi	reason for the decison
Res ipsa loquitur	the thing speaks for itself
Stare decisis	to stand by past decisions
Sui juris	of legal capacity
Tortfeasor	one liable for a civil wrong, except re. contract or trust matters
Uberrimae fidei	of the utmost good faith
Ultra vires	beyond one's powers
Volenti non fit injuria	no wrong can be done to one who consents to the action

Index 1

Index 3